joni mitchell
hits

Arrangements by Hemme Luttjeboer
and Dylan Schorer based on Transcriptions
by Joel Bernstein

Dulcimer Transcriptions by Joellen Lapidus
and Ruth Barrett

Special Thanks To Joel Bernstein for his
editorial assistance.

Project Managers: Carol Cuellar & Aaron Stang
Photography: Norman Seeff
Cover Photo: Baron Wolman
Art Layout: Robbie Cavolina

Urge For Going

I awoke today and found the frost
perched on the town
It hovered in a frozen sky, then it
gobbled summer down
When the sun turns traitor cold and all
the trees are shivering in a naked row

I get the urge for going
But I never seem to go
I get the urge for going
When the meadow grass is turning brown
Summertime is falling down and winter
is closing in

I had me a man in summertime
He had summer-colored skin
And not another girl in town
My darling's heart could win
But when the leaves fell on the ground
Boy winds came around, pushed them face down in the snow

He got the urge for going
And I had to let him go
He got the urge for going
When the meadow grass was turning brown
Summertime was falling down and winter was closing in

Now the warriors of winter they gave a cold triumphant shout
And all that stays is dying and all that lives is camping out
See the geese in chevron flight flapping and racing on before the snow

They got the urge for going
And they got the wings so they can go
They get the urge for going
When the meadow grass is turning brown
Summertime is falling down and winter
is closing in

Apply the fire with kindling now
I'll pull the blankets up to my chin
I'll lock the vagrant winter out and I'll fold my wandering in
I'd like to call back summertime
Have her stay for just another
month or so

But she's got the urge for going
So I guess she'll have to go
She gets the urge for going
When the meadow grass is turning brown
All her empire's falling down
And winter's closing in
And I get the urge for going
When the meadow grass is turning brown
And summertime is falling down

©1966, Copyright Renewed, Crazy Crow Music (BMI)

Chelsea Morning

Woke up, it was a Chelsea morning, and the first thing that I heard
Was a song outside my window, and the traffic wrote the words
It came ringing up like Christmas bells, and rapping up
like pipes and drums

Oh, won't you stay
We'll put on the day
And we'll wear it till the night comes

Woke up, it was a Chelsea morning, and the first thing that I saw
Was the sun through yellow curtains, and a rainbow on the wall
Blue, red, green and gold to welcome you, crimson crystal
beads to beckon

Oh, won't you stay
We'll put on the day
There's a sun show every second

Now the curtain opens on a
portrait of today
And the streets are paved with passersby
And pigeons fly
And papers lie
Waiting to blow away

Woke up, it was a Chelsea morning, and the first thing that I knew
There was milk and toast and honey and a bowl of oranges, too
And the sun poured in like butterscotch and stuck to all my senses

Oh, won't you stay
We'll put on the day
And we'll talk in present tenses

When the curtain closes and the
rainbow runs away
I will bring you incense owls by night
By candlelight
By jewel-light
If only you will stay
Pretty baby, won't you
Woke up, it's a Chelsea morning

©1967, Copyright Renewed, Crazy Crow Music (BMI)

Big Yellow Taxi

They paved paradise
And put up a parking lot
With a pink hotel, a boutique
And a swinging hot spot
Don't it always seem to go
That you don't know what you've got
Till it's gone
They paved paradise
And put up a parking lot
They took all the trees
And put them in a tree museum

And they charged the people
A dollar and a half just to see 'em
Don't it always seem to go

That you don't know what you've got
Till it's gone
They paved paradise
And put up a parking lot

Hey farmer farmer
Put away that D.D.T. now
Give me spots on my apples
But leave me the birds and the bees
Please!
Don't it always seem to go
That you don't know what you've got
Till it's gone
They paved paradise
And put up a parking lot

Late last night
I heard the screen door slam
And a big yellow taxi
Took away my old man
Don't it always seem to go
That you don't know what you've got
Till it's gone
They paved paradise
And put up a parking lot

©1970 Siquomb Publishing Corp. (BMI)

Woodstock

I came upon a child of God
He was walking along the road
And I asked him, where are you going
And this he told me
I'm going on down to Yasgur's farm
I'm going to join in a
rock 'n' roll band
I'm going to camp out on the land
I'm going to try an' get my soul free
We are stardust
We are golden
And we've got to get ourselves
Back to the garden

Then can I walk beside you
I have come here to lose the smog
And I feel to be a cog in
something turning
Well maybe it is just the time of year
Or maybe it's the time of man
I don't know who I am
But life is for learning
We are stardust
We are golden
And we've got to get ourselves
Back to the garden

By the time we got to Woodstock
We were half a million strong
And everywhere there was song
and celebration
And I dreamed I saw the bombers
Riding shotgun in the sky
And they were turning into butterflies
Above our nation
We are stardust
We are golden
And we've got to get ourselves
Back to the garden

©1969 Siquomb Publishing Corp. (BMI)

The Circle Game

Yesterday a child came out to wonder
Caught a dragonfly inside a jar
Fearful when the sky was full of thunder
And tearful at the falling of a star

chorus:
And the seasons they go round and round
And the painted ponies go up and down
We're captive on the carousel of time
We can't return, we can only look behind
From where we came
And go round and round and round
In the circle game

Then the child moved ten times
round the seasons
Skated over ten clear frozen streams
Words like "when you're older"
must appease him
And promises of someday make his dreams

chorus

Sixteen springs and sixteen
summers gone now
Cartwheels turn to car wheels
through the town
And they tell him, "take your time,

Urge For Going

I awoke today and found the frost
perched on the town
It hovered in a frozen sky, then it
gobbled summer down
When the sun turns traitor cold and all
the trees are shivering in a naked row

I get the urge for going
But I never seem to go
I get the urge for going
When the meadow grass is turning brown
Summertime is falling down and winter
is closing in

I had me a man in summertime
He had summer-colored skin
And not another girl in town
My darling's heart could win
But when the leaves fell on the ground
Bully winds came around, pushed them face down in the snow

He got the urge for going
And I had to let him go
He got the urge for going
When the meadow grass was turning brown
Summertime was falling down and winter was closing in

Now the warriors of winter they gave a cold triumphant shout
And all that stays is dying and all that lives is getting out
See the geese in chevron flight flapping and racing on before the snow

They got the urge for going
And they got the wings so they can go
They get the urge for going
When the meadow grass is turning brown
Summertime is falling down and winter
is closing in

Apply the fire with kindling now
I'll pull the blankets up to my chin
I'll look the vagrant winter out and I'll fold my wandering in
I'd like to call back summertime
Have her stay for just another
month or so

But she's got the urge for going
So I guess she'll have to go
She gets the urge for going
When the meadow grass is turning brown
All her empire's falling down
And winter's closing in
And I get the urge for going
When the meadow grass is turning brown
And summertime is falling down

©1966, Copyright Renewed, Crazy Crow Music (BMI)

Chelsea Morning

Woke up, it was a Chelsea morning, and the first thing that I heard
Was a song outside my window, and the traffic wrote the words
It came ringing up like Christmas bells, and rapping up
like pipes and drums

Oh, won't you stay
We'll put on the day
And we'll wear it till the night comes

Woke up, it was a Chelsea morning, and the first thing that I saw
Was the sun through yellow curtains, and a rainbow on the wall
Blue, red, green and gold to welcome you, crimson crystal
beads to beckon

Oh, won't you stay
We'll put on the day
There's a sun show every second

Now the curtain opens on a
portrait of today
And the streets are paved with passersby
And pigeons fly
And papers lie
Waiting to blow away

Woke up, it was a Chelsea morning, and the first thing that I knew
There was milk and toast and honey and a bowl of oranges, too
And the sun poured in like butterscotch and stuck to all my senses

Oh, won't you stay
We'll put on the day
And we'll talk in present tenses

When the curtain closes and the
rainbow runs away
I will bring you incense owls by night
By candlelight
By jewel-light
If only you will stay
Pretty baby, won't you
Woke up, it's a Chelsea morning

©1967, Copyright Renewed, Crazy Crow Music (BMI)

Big Yellow Taxi

They paved paradise
And put up a parking lot
With a pink hotel, a boutique
And a swinging hot spot
Don't it always seem to go
That you don't know what you've got

Till it's gone
They paved paradise
And put up a parking lot
They took all the trees
And put them in a tree museum

And they charged the people
A dollar and a half just to see 'em
Don't it always seem to go

That you don't know what you've got
Till it's gone
They paved paradise
And put up a parking lot

Hey farmer farmer
Put away that D.D.T. now
Give me spots on my apples
But leave me the birds and the bees
Please!
Don't it always seem to go
That you don't know what you've got
Till it's gone
They paved paradise
And put up a parking lot

Late last night
I heard the screen door slam
And a big yellow taxi
Took away my old man
Don't it always seem to go
That you don't know what you've got
Till it's gone
They paved paradise
And put up a parking lot

©1970 Siquomb Publishing Corp. (BMI)

Woodstock

I came upon a child of God
He was walking along the road
And I asked him, where are you going
And this he told me
I'm going on down to Yasgur's farm
I'm going to join in a
rock 'n' roll band
I'm going to camp out on the land
I'm going to try an' get my soul free
We are stardust
We are golden
And we've got to get ourselves
Back to the garden

Then can I walk beside you
I have come here to lose the smog
And I feel to be a cog in
something turning
Well maybe it is just the time of year
Or maybe it's the time of man
I don't know who I am
But life is for learning
We are stardust
We are golden
And we've got to get ourselves
Back to the garden

By the time we got to Woodstock
We were half a million strong
And everywhere there was song
and celebration
And I dreamed I saw the bombers
Riding shotgun in the sky
And they were turning into butterflies
Above our nation
We are stardust
We are golden
And we've got to get ourselves
Back to the garden

©1969 Siquomb Publishing Corp. (BMI)

The Circle Game

Yesterday a child came out to wonder
Caught a dragonfly inside a jar
Fearful when the sky was full of thunder
And tearful at the falling of a star

chorus:
And the seasons they go round and round
And the painted ponies go up and down
We're captive on the carousel of time
We can't return, we can only look behind
From where we came
And go round and round and round
In the circle game

Then the child moved ten times
round the seasons
Skated over ten clear frozen streams
Words like "when you're older"
must appease him
And promises of someday make his dreams

chorus

Sixteen springs and sixteen
summers gone now
Cartwheels turn to car wheels
through the town
And they tell him, "take your time,

Gin's what I'm drinking
I was raised on robbery

I'm a pretty good cook
I'm sitting on my groceries
Come up to my kitchen
I'll show you my best recipe
I try and I try but I can't save a cent
I'm up after midnight cooking
Trying to make my rent
I'm rough but I'm pleasin'
I was raised on robbery

We had a little money once
They were pushing through a
four-lane highway
Government gave us three
thousand dollars
You should have seen it fly away
First he bought a '57 Biscayne
He put it in the ditch
He drunk up all the rest
That son of a bitch
His blood's bad whiskey
I was raised on robbery

You know you ain't bad looking
I like the way you hold your drinks
Come home with me honey
I ain't asking for no full-length mink
Hey, where you going...

Don't go yet...
Your glass ain't empty and we just met
You're mean when you're loaded—
I was raised on robbery"

©1973 Crazy Crow Music (BMI)

Help Me

Help me
I think I'm falling
In love again
When I get that crazy feeling, I know
I'm in trouble again
I'm in trouble
'Cause you're a rambler and a gambler
And a sweet-talking ladies man
And you love your lovin'
But not like you love your freedom

Help me
I think I'm falling
In love too fast
It's got me hoping for the future
And worrying about the past
'Cause I've seen some hot hot blazes
Come down to smoke and ash
We love our lovin'
But not like we love our freedom

Didn't it feel good
We were sitting there talking
Or lying there not talking
Didn't it feel good
You dance with the lady
With the hole in her stocking
Didn't it feel good
Didn't it feel good

Help me
I think I'm falling
In love with you
Are you going to let me go
there by myself
That's such a lonely thing to do
Both of us flirting around
Flirting and flirting
Hurting too
We love our lovin'
But not like we love our freedom

©1973 Crazy Crow Music (BMI)

Free Man In Paris

"The way I see it," he said,
"You just can't win it
Everybody's in it for their own gain
You can't please 'em all
There's always somebody calling you down
I do my best
And I do good business
There's a lot of people asking
for my time
They're trying to get ahead
They're trying to be a good
friend of mine

I was a free man in Paris
I felt unfettered and alive
There was nobody calling me
up for favors
And no one's future to decide
You know I'd go back there tomorrow
But for the work I've taken on
Stoking the star maker machinery
Behind the popular song

I deal in dreamers
And telephone screamers

Lately I wonder what I do it for
If I had my way
I'd just walk through those doors
And wander
Down the Champs Elysées
Going café to cabaret
Thinking how I'll feel when I find
That very good friend of mine

I was a free man in Paris
I felt unfettered and alive
Nobody was calling me up for favors
No one's future to decide
You know I'd go back there tomorrow
But for the work I've taken on
Stoking the star maker machinery
Behind the popular song"

©1973 Crazy Crow Music (BMI)

River

It's coming on Christmas
They're cutting down trees
They're putting up reindeer
And singing songs of joy and peace
Oh I wish I had a river
I could skate away on
But it don't snow here
It stays pretty green
I'm going to make a lot of money
Then I'm going to quit this crazy scene
I wish I had a river
I could skate away on
I wish I had a river so long
I would teach my feet to fly
Oh I wish I had a river
I could skate away on
I made my baby cry

He tried hard to help me
You know, he put me at ease
And he loved me so naughty
Made me weak in the knees
Oh I wish I had a river
I could skate away on
I'm so hard to handle
I'm selfish and I'm sad
Now I've gone and lost the best baby
That I ever had
Oh I wish I had a river
I could skate away on
I wish I had a river so long
I would teach my feet to fly
Oh I wish I had a river
I could skate away on
I made my baby say goodbye

It's coming on Christmas
They're cutting down trees
They're putting up reindeer
Singing songs of joy and peace
I wish I had a river
I could skate away on

©1971 Joni Mitchell Publishing Corp. (BMI)

Chinese Café/Unchained Melody

Caught in the middle
Carol, we're middle class
We're middle aged
We were wild in the old days
Birth of rock 'n' roll days
Now your kids are coming up straight
And my child's a stranger
I bore her
But I could not raise her
Nothing lasts for long
Nothing lasts for long
Nothing lasts for long
Down at the Chinese Café
We'd be dreaming on our dimes
We'd be playing—
"Oh my love, my darling"
One more time

Uranium money
Is booming in the old home town now
Putting up sleek concrete
Tearing the old landmarks down
Paving over brave little parks
Ripping off Indian land again
How long—how long
Short-sighted businessmen
Ah, nothing lasts for long
Nothing lasts for long
Nothing lasts for long
Down at the Chinese Café
We'd be dreaming on our dimes
We'd be playing—
"You give your love so sweetly"
One more time

Christmas is sparkling
Out on Carol's lawn
This girl of my childhood games
Has kids nearly grown and gone
Grown so fast
Like the turn of a page

We look like our mothers did now
When we were those kids' age
Nothing lasts for long
Nothing lasts for long
Nothing lasts for long
Down at the Chinese Café
We'd be dreaming on our dimes
We'd be playing—

"Oh my love, my darling
I've hungered for your touch
A long lonely time
And time goes by so slowly
And time can do so much
Are you still mine?
I need your love
I need your love
God speed your love to me"
(Time goes—where does the time go—
I wonder where the time goes...)

Come In From The Cold

Way back in 1957
We had to dance a foot apart
And they hawk-eyed us
From the sidelines
Holding their rulers without a heart
And so with just a touch of our fingers
Oh, we could make our circuitry explode
All we ever wanted
Was just to come in from the cold

Come in
Come in from the cold
(we were so young)
Oh come in
Come in from the cold

We really thought we had a purpose
We were so anxious to achieve
We had hope
The world held promise
For a slave
To liberty

Freely I slaved away for
something better
And I was bought and sold
And all I ever wanted
Was just to come in from the cold

Come in
Come in from the cold
(we were so sure)
Please come in
Come in from the cold

I feel your legs under the table
Leaning into mine
I feel renewed
I feel disabled
By these bonfires in my spine
I don't know who the arsonist was
Which incendiary soul
But all I ever wanted
Was just to come in from the cold

Come in
Come in from the cold
(you were too warm)
Oh come in come in
Come in from the cold

I am not some stone commission
Like a statue in a park
I am flesh and blood and vision
I am howling in the dark
Long blue shadows of the jackals
Are falling on a pay phone
By the road
Oh all we ever wanted
Was just to come in from the cold

Come in
Come in from the cold
(i was so low)
Oh come in
Come in from the cold

Is this just vulgar electricity
Is this the edifying fire
(it was so pure)
Does your smile's covert complicity
Debase as it admires
(just a flu with a temperature)
Are you just checking out your mojo
Or am I just fighting off growing old
(just a high fever)
All I ever wanted
Was just to come in from the cold

Come in
Come in from the cold
(it was so pure)
Please come in
Come in from the cold

I know we never will be perfect
Never entirely clear
(when the moon shines)
We get hurt and we just panic
And we strike out
Out of fear
(you were only being kind)
I fear the sentence of this solitude
200 years on hold
(for my loving crime)
Oh and all we ever wanted
Was just to come in from the cold

Come in
Oh come in from the cold
(when the moon shines)
Oh come in
Come in from the cold

When I thought life had some meaning
Then I thought I had some choice
(i was running blind)
And I made some value judgments
In a self-important voice
(i was outa line)
But then absurdity came over me
And I longed to lose control
(into no mind)
Oh all I ever wanted
Was just to come in from the cold

Come in
Come in from the cold
(you were so kind)
Please come in
(so kind)
Come in from the cold
Come in come in
Come in from the cold

Both Sides, Now

Rows and flows of angel hair
And ice cream castles in the air
And feather canyons ev'rywhere
I've looked at clouds that way

But now they only block the sun
They rain and snow on ev'ryone
So many things I would have done
But clouds got in my way

I've looked at clouds from
both sides now
From up and down, and still somehow

It's cloud illusions I recall
I really don't know clouds at all

Moons and Junes and Ferris wheels
The dizzy dancing way you feel
As ev'ry fairy tale comes real
I've looked at love that way

But now it's just another show
You leave 'em laughing when you go
And if you care, don't let them know
Don't give yourself away

I've looked at love from both sides now
From give and take, and still somehow
It's love's illusions I recall
I really don't know love at all

Tears and fears and feeling proud
To say "I love you" right out loud
Dreams and schemes and circus crowds
I've looked at life that way

But now old friends are acting strange
They shake their heads, they say
I've changed
Well something's lost, but
something's gained
In living ev'ry day

I've looked at life from both sides now
From win and lose and still somehow
It's life's illusions I recall
I really don't know life at all

I've looked at life from both sides now
From up and down, and still somehow
It's life's illusions I recall
I really don't know life at all

Joni Mitchell and The Guitar

Although Joni Mitchell is by no means the first songwriter to compose on the guitar using non-standard tunings, it can be reasonably claimed that she has explored the world of these tunings, and particularly that of non-standard/non-open tunings, to a greater depth than any composer that came before her. These explorations began in the mid-60s, when she first learned of, and started composing in, conventional open tunings such as open D [DADF#AD], E (same tuning-one whole step up [EBEG#BE]), and G [DGDGBD], as well as other common alternate tunings, such as "D Modal" [DADGBD]. While tuning her guitar from one open tuning to another she came upon unlooked-for intermediate chords whose tone-color immediately resonated with her. She thus began to compose in tunings that had never been explored before; each one opening a new window upon guitar composition. Her use of these unique non-standard tunings became the most recognized trademark of her guitar style. Now, some 30 years later, she has written compositions in over 40 different tunings (not counting tunings duplicated in other keys). In this volume are presented full chord frame and tablature arrangements of the songs included in her recent compilation "Hits"; it is hoped that these transcriptions will not only enable guitarists to play these songs as they were composed, but will also inspire them to carry out their own explorations in this still-fertile territory.

Joel Bernstein

Joni Mitchell and The Dulcimer

Joni Mitchell discovered and bought her first dulcimer at the 1967 Big Sur Folk Festival. During the folk revival of the 1960s, Appalachian singer and folk musician Jean Richie introduced a whole generation of Americans to this traditional modal American folk instrument that was always played with open tunings. Experimenting with every conceivable style under the sun, the next generation of American dulcimer players expanded the repertoire of the dulcimer and played classical, rock, jazz, East Indian music and more on this versatile instrument. Even before Joni Mitchell discovered the dulcimer, without knowing it, she had already affected this new generation of dulcimer players through her open guitar tunings and fluid rhythms. When she bought her first dulcimer, she was taught how to play by someone who had already been influenced by her music. She wrote four dulcimer songs which appeared on her BLUE album, quickly becoming classics for all contemporary dulcimer players.

Note: Joni strings her dulcimer with the bass strings in the center. Our tablature and tuning instructions put the bass strings on top which is traditional. Since the tuning is the same, the sound and chord voicings will be identical.

Joellen Lapidus
Ruth Barrett

URGE FOR GOING

Words and Music by
JONI MITCHELL

Standard tuning, Capo 3rd fret

Moderately ♩ = 114

Intro:

hold throughout

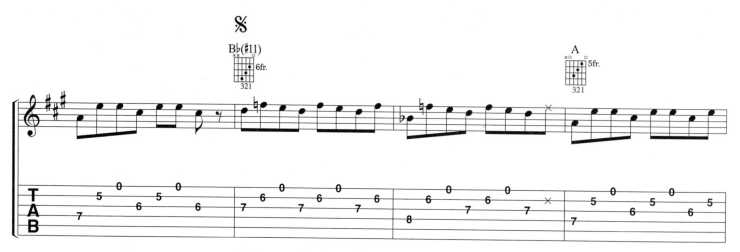

Gtr. 2 enters, loosely doubling Gtr. 1 throughout.

Verses 1 & 4:

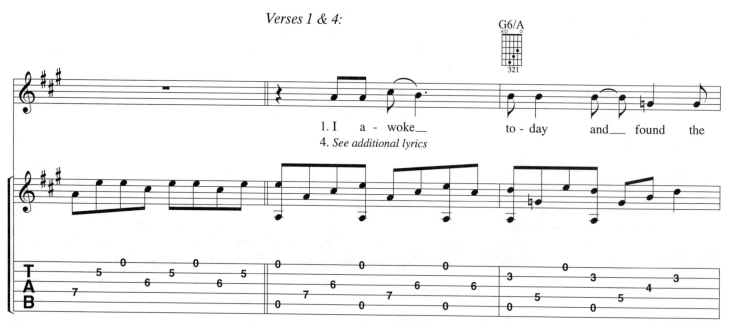

1. I a - woke___ to - day and___ found the
4. *See additional lyrics*

Urge for Going - 8 - 1
PG9666

frost perched on____ the town.____   It hov - ered in_____ a fro -

zen____ sky,   then it____ gob - bled sum - mer down.____

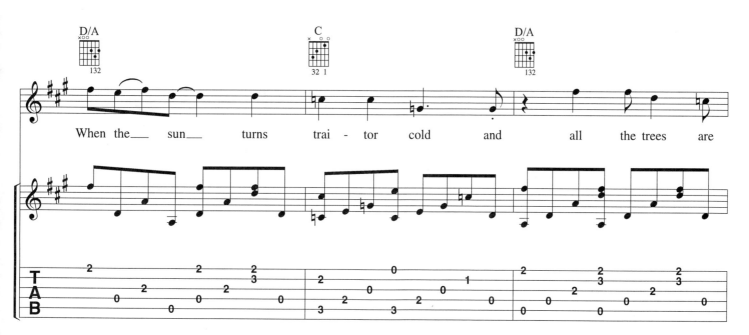

When the____ sun____ turns trai - tor cold and   all the trees are

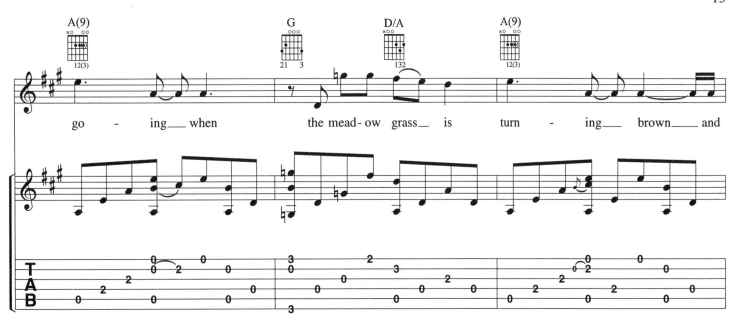

go - ing___ when   the mead-ow grass___ is   turn - ing___ brown___ and

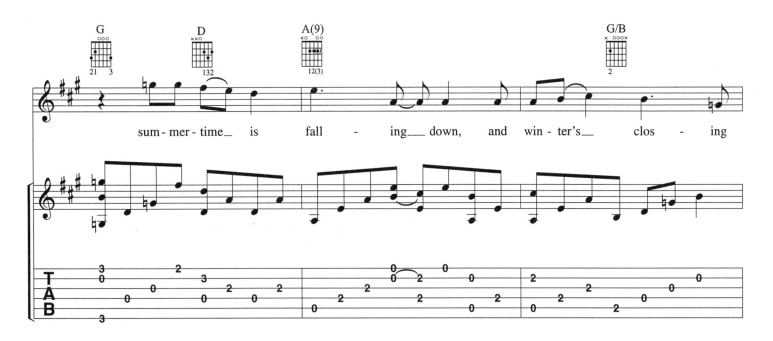

sum-mer-time___ is   fall - ing___ down,   and win - ter's___   clos - ing

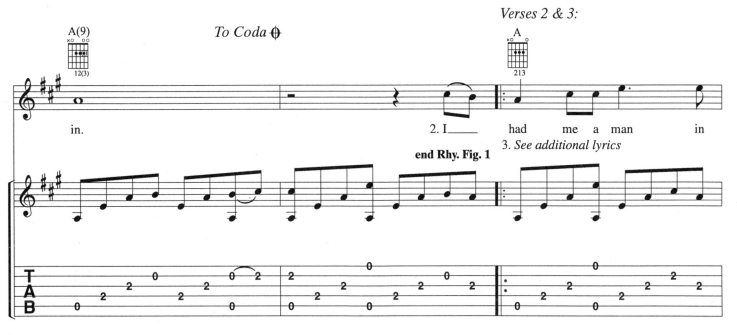

in.

Verses 2 & 3:

2. I___ had   me a man   in
3. *See additional lyrics*

end Rhy. Fig. 1

To Coda

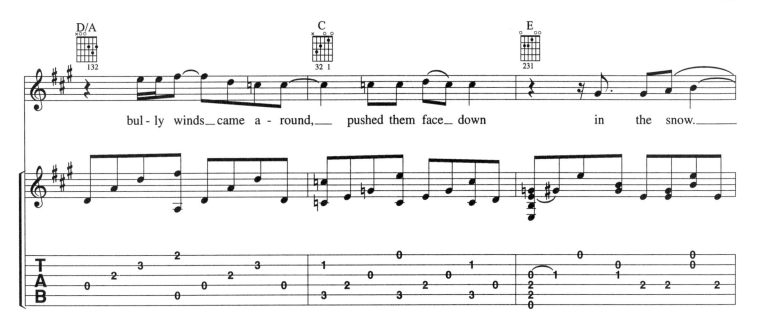

bul - ly winds__ came a - round,__ pushed them face__ down   in   the   snow.__

Chorus 2 & 3:

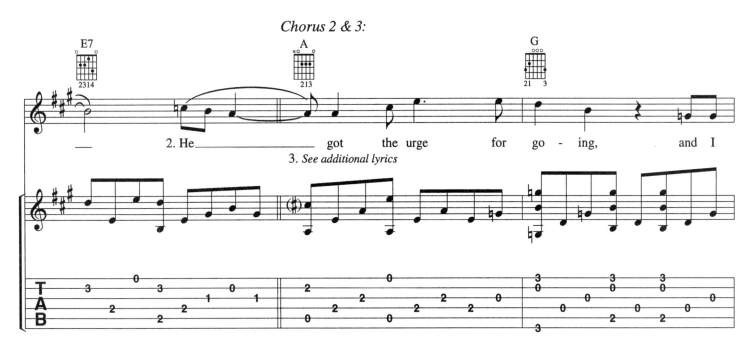

2. He_____ got   the   urge   for   go - ing,   and   I
3. See additional lyrics

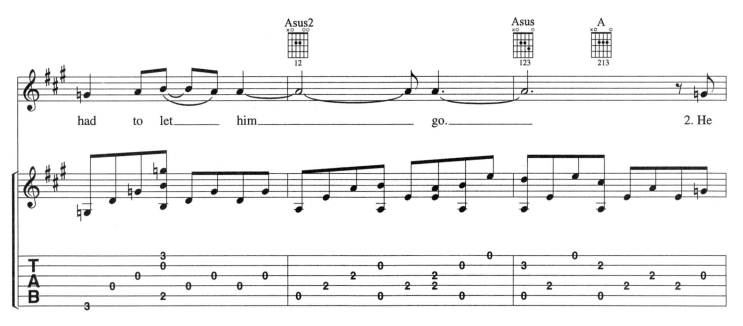

had   to   let____ him_____   go._____   2. He

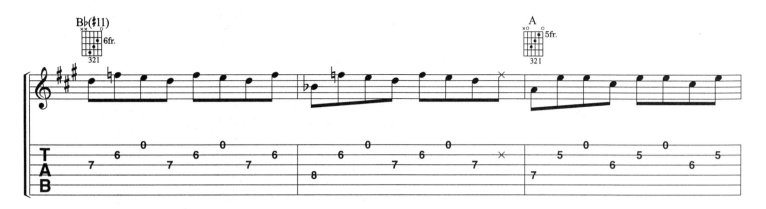

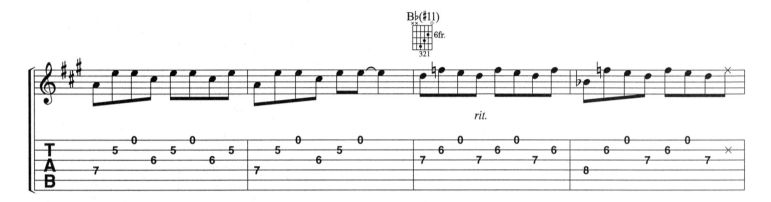

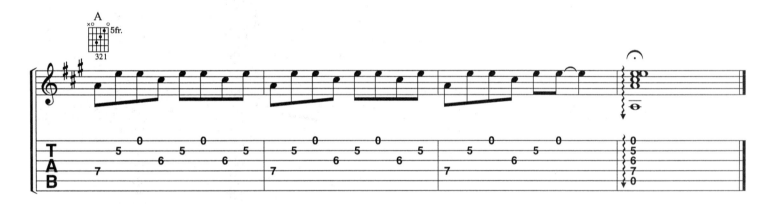

Verse 3:
Now the warriors of winter, they give a cold triumphant shout.
And all that stays is dyin', all that lives is gettin' out.
See the geese in chevron flight,
Flappin' and a-racin' on before the snow.

Chorus 3:
They got the urge for going and they've got the wings so they can go.
They get the urge for going when the meadow grass is turning brown and
Summertime is falling down, and winter's closing in.

Verse 4:
I'll ply the fire with kindling now, I'll pull the blankets up to my chin.
I'll lock the vagrant winter out, and I'll bolt my wandering in.
I'd like to call back summertime
And have her stay for just another month or so,

Chorus 4:
But she's got the urge for going, so I guess she'll have to go.
She gets the urge for going when the meadow grass is turning brown
And all her empire's fallen down, and winter's closing in.

CHELSEA MORNING

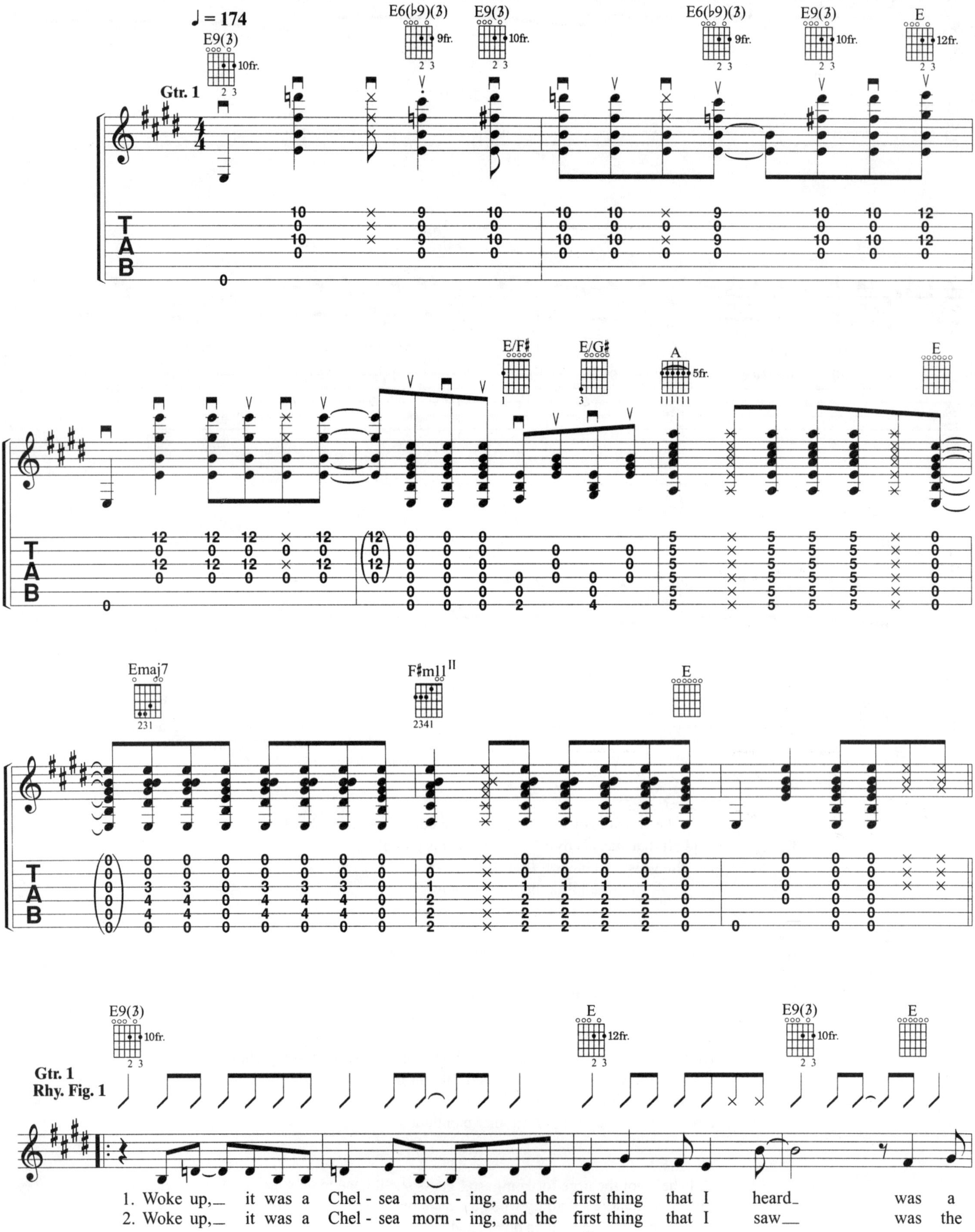

Gtr. 1 tuning:
⑥ = E ③ = G♯
⑤ = B ② = B
④ = E ① = E

Words and Music by
JONI MITCHELL

♩ = 174
E9(♮3) E6(♭9)(♮3) E9(♮3) E6(♭9)(♮3) E9(♮3) E
Gtr. 1
E/F♯ E/G♯ A E
Emaj7 F♯m11 E
E9(♮3) E E9(♮3) E
Gtr. 1
Rhy. Fig. 1
1. Woke up, it was a Chel - sea morn - ing, and the first thing that I heard was a
2. Woke up, it was a Chel - sea morn - ing, and the first thing that I saw was the

19

BIG YELLOW TAXI

Words and Music by
JONI MITCHELL

Gtr. tuning:
⑥ = E ③ = G#
⑤ = B ② = B
④ = E ① = E

Moderately fast ♩ = 172

Intro:

Gtr. 1

1. They paved par-a-dise, put up a park-ing lot,
2.3.4. *See additional lyrics*

with a pink ho - tel,___ a

bou - tique, and a swing - ing hot___ spot.___

Big Yellow Taxi - 3 - 1
PG9666

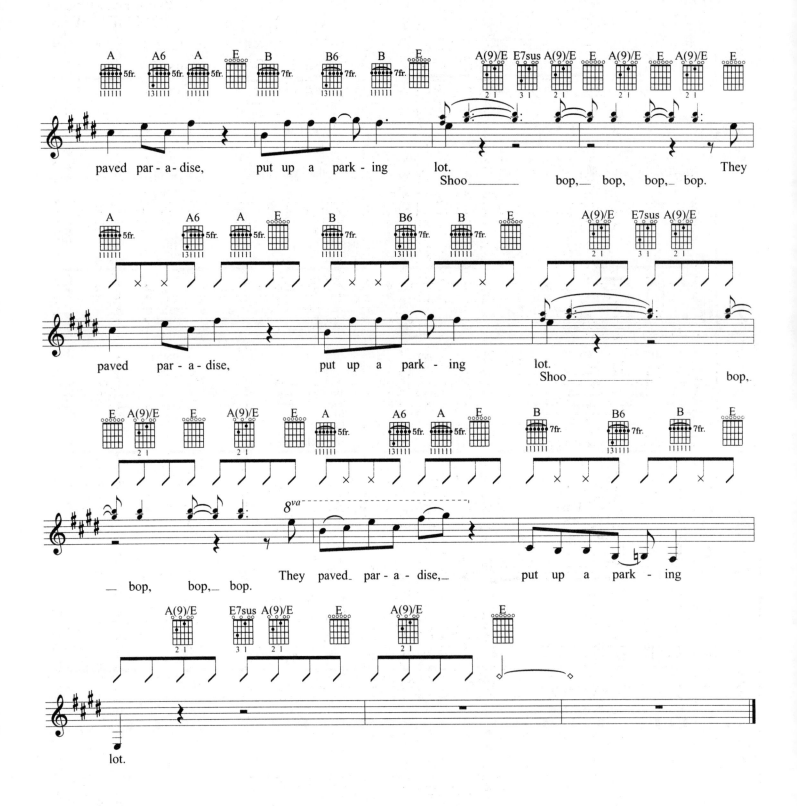

Verse 2:
They took all the trees,
Put them in a tree museum.
And they charged all the people
A dollar and a half just to see 'em.
(To Chorus:)

Verse 3:
Hey farmer, farmer,
Put away the D.D.T., now.
Give me spots on all my apples,
But leave me the birds and the bees.
Please!
(To Chorus:)

Verse 4:
Late last night,
I heard the screen door slam,
And a big yellow taxi
Took away my old man.
(To Chorus:)

WOODSTOCK

Words and Music by
JONI MITCHELL

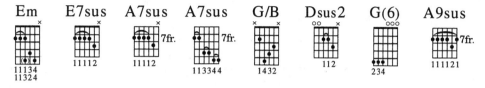

Tune Gtr. 1 down:
⑥ = D♭   ③ = G♭
⑤ = A♭   ② = B♭
④ = D♭   ① = E♭

Freely
Intro:

*Electric piano arranged for gtr.

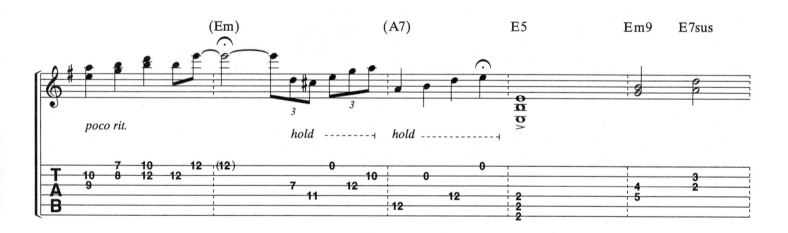

Moderately ♩ = ca. 108

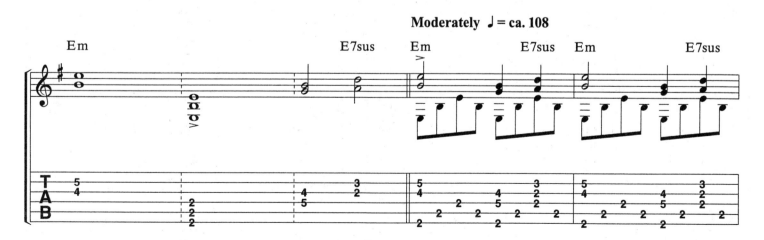

Woodstock - 9 - 1
PG9666

1. I

Verse:

came up - on___ a child___ of God.___ He was walk-ing a-long___ the

2. 3. See additional lyrics

Rhy. Fig. 1

road and I asked him,___ "Where are you go - ing?"___ and this

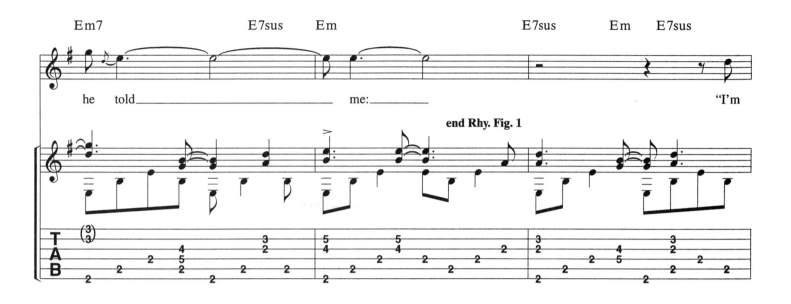

Chorus:

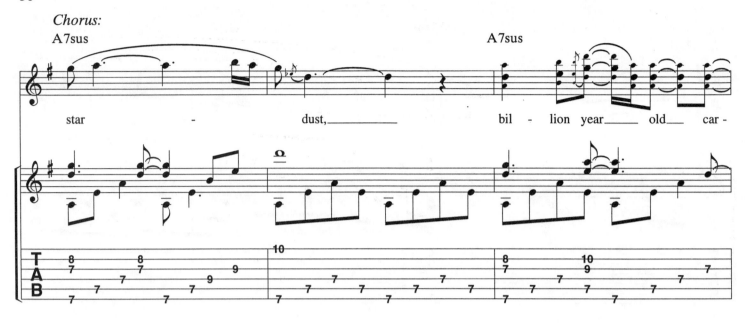

star - dust,_____ bil - lion year____ old____ car -

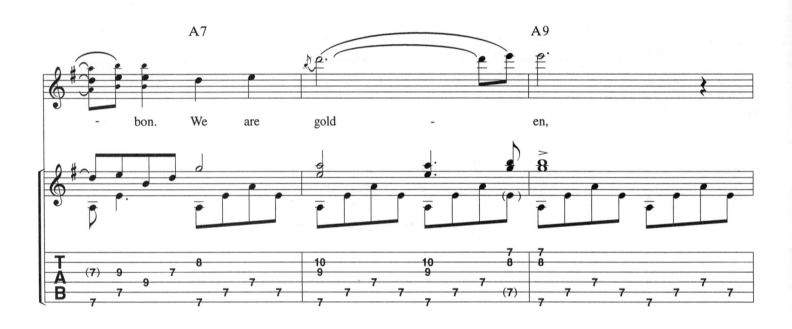

- bon. We are gold - en,

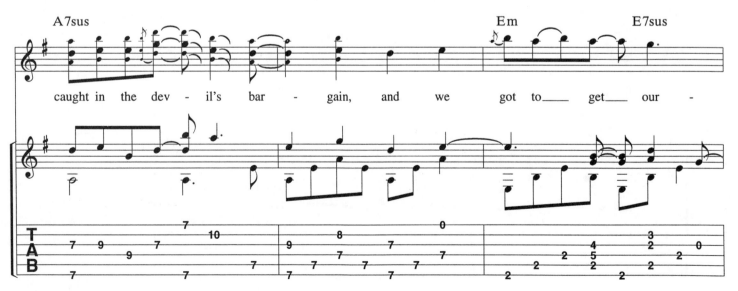

caught in the dev - il's bar - gain, and we got to____ get____ our -

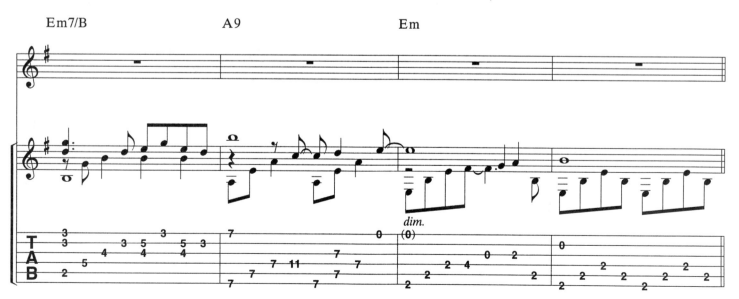

Woodstock - 9 - 7

PG9666

Slower
Outro:

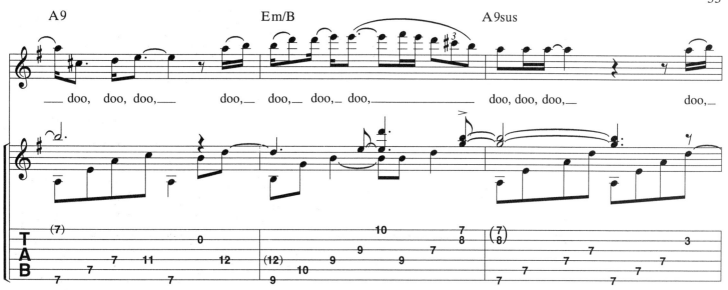

*Left-hand tap.
**Right-hand tap.

Verse 2:
Then can I walk beside you?
I have come here to lose the smog.
And I feel to be a cog
In something turning.
Well, maybe it is just the time of year,
Or maybe it's the time of man.
I don't know who I am,
But, you know, life is for learning.
(To Chorus:)

Verse 3:
By the time we got to Woodstock,
We were half a million strong,
And everywhere was song and celebration.
And I dreamed I saw the bombers
Riding shotgun in the sky,
And they were turning into butterflies
Above our nation.

THE CIRCLE GAME

Words and Music by
JONI MITCHELL

Gtr. 1 tune to and capo 4th fret:

⑥ = D ③ = G
⑤ = G ② = B
④ = D ① = D

Moderately fast ♩ = 120

Intro:

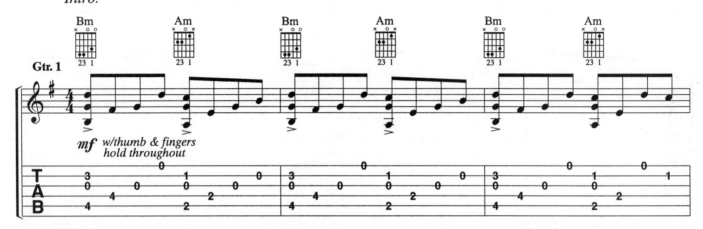

*Basic harmony.

Verses:

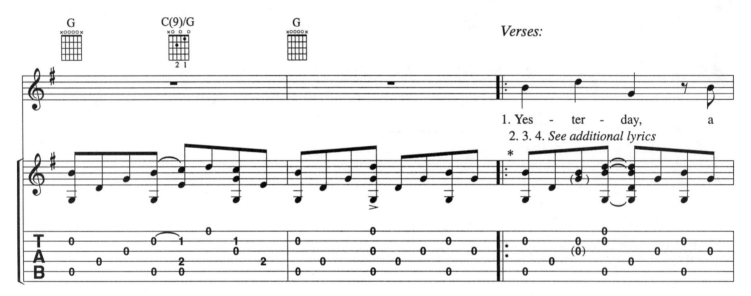

1. Yes - ter - day, a
2. 3. 4. *See additional lyrics*

*Gtr. 1 dbld. by 2nd acoustic gtr.,
arranged here for one gtr.

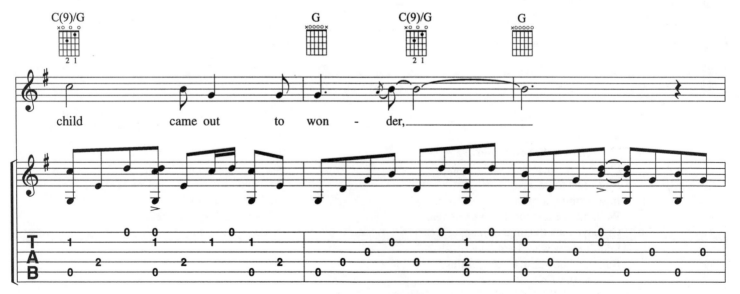

child   came out   to won - der,_____

The Circle Game - 5 - 1
PG9666

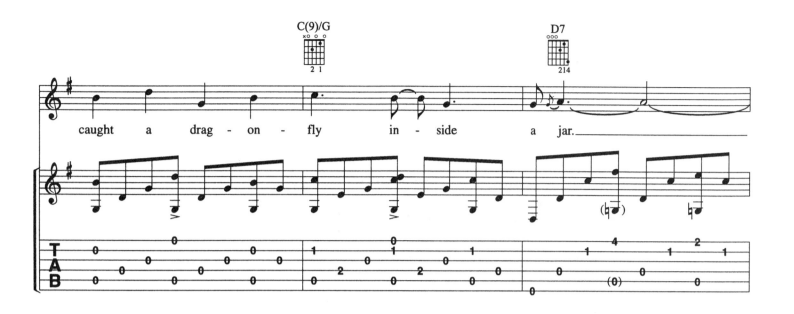

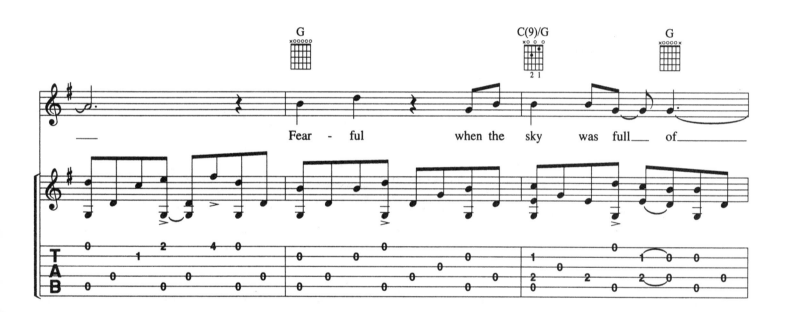

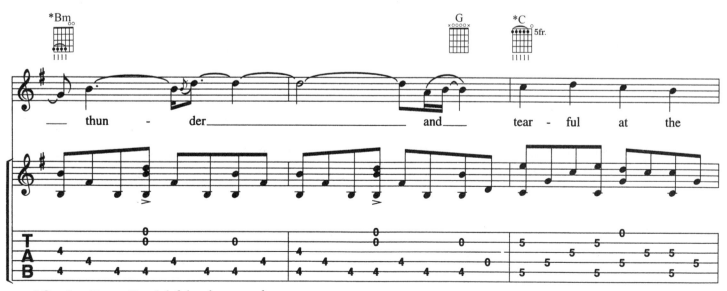

* Overhand barre. Reach left hand **over** neck.

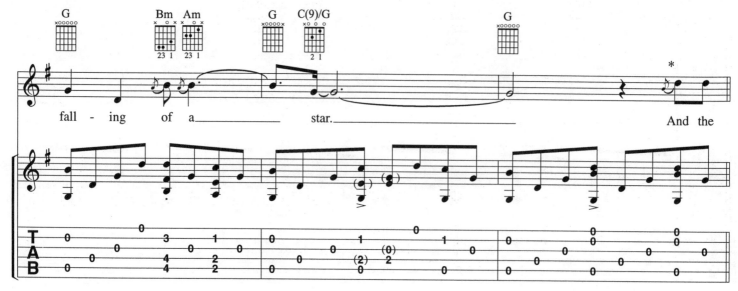

fall - ing of a_____ star._____ And the

*Vocals dbld. 8vb and unison.

Chorus:

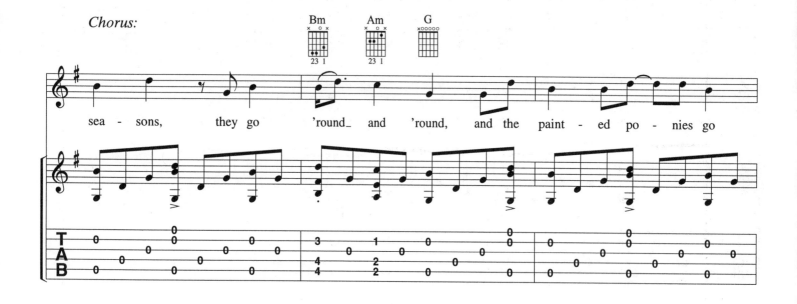

sea - sons, they go 'round_ and 'round, and the paint - ed po - nies go

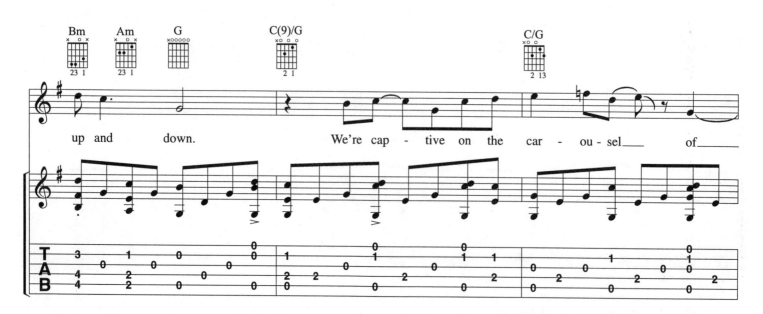

up and down. We're cap - tive on the car - ou - sel___ of_____

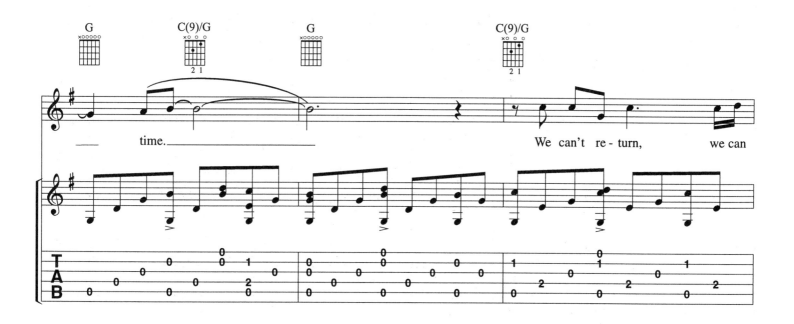

time._____ We can't re-turn, we can

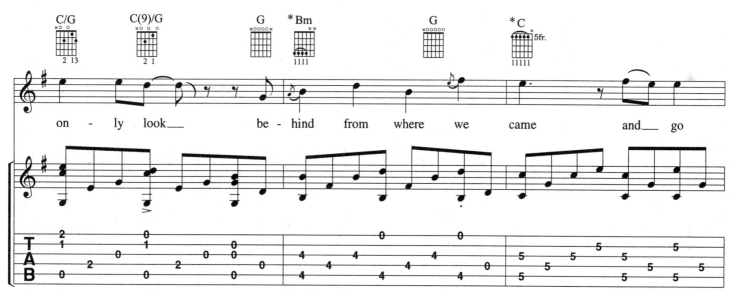

on-ly look___ be-hind from where we came and___ go

* Overhand barre. Reach left hand **over** neck.

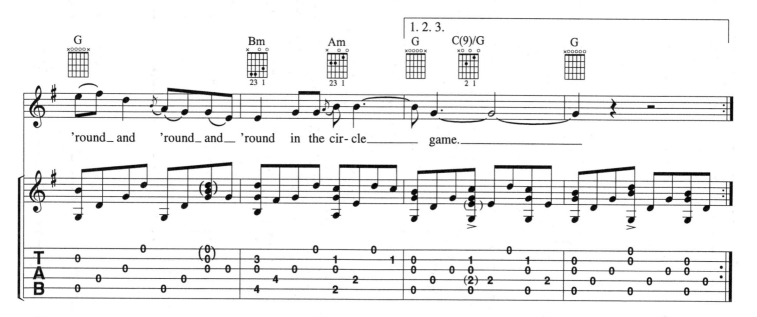

'round_ and 'round_ and_ 'round in the cir-cle_____ game._____

The Circle Game - 5 - 4
PG9666

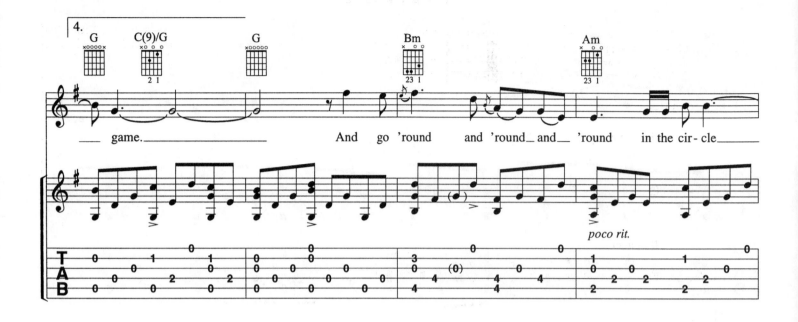

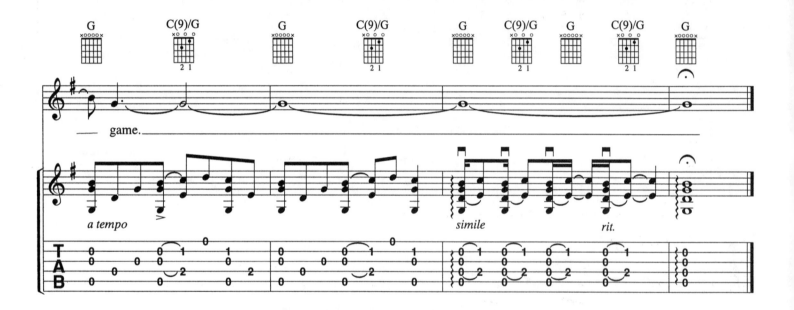

Verse 2:
Then the child moved ten times 'round the seasons,
Skated over ten clear frozen streams.
Words like, "When you're older," must appease him,
And promises of someday make his dreams...
(To Chorus:)

Verse 3:
Sixteen springs and sixteen summers gone now,
Cartwheels turn to car wheels through the town.
And they tell him, "Take your time, it won't be long now,
Till you drag your feet to slow the circles down"...
(To Chorus:)

Verse 4:
So the years spin by and now the boy is twenty;
Though his dreams have lost some grandeur coming true,
There'll be new dreams, maybe better dreams and plenty,
Before the last revolving year is through...
(To Chorus:)

CAREY

**Words and Music by
JONI MITCHELL**

Gtr. 1 tune to:
⑥ = D ③ = G
⑤ = A ② = A
④ = D ① = D

Dulcimer tune to:
BASS = D
MIDDLE = A
DOUBLE = A

*(To match record, tune to DADGAD,
then down 1/2 step)

Moderately in 2 ♩ = 78
Intro:

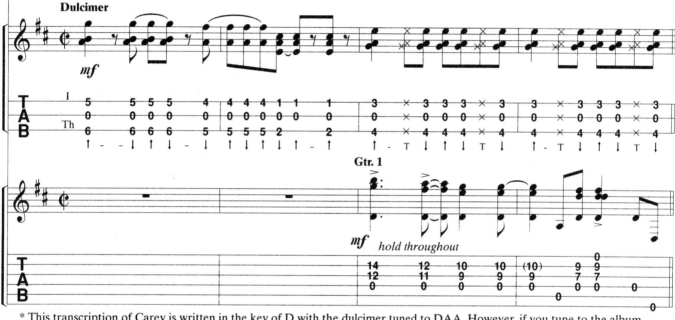

* This transcription of Carey is written in the key of D with the dulcimer tuned to DAA. However, if you tune to the album, you will find the dulcimer and guitars are tuned 1/2 step flat.

Verses 1, 2, & 3:

wind is in from Af - ri - ca.__ Last night, I could - n't sleep.__ Oh, you know it

2.3. *See additional lyrics*

Carey - 7 - 1
PG9666

42

Verse 4:

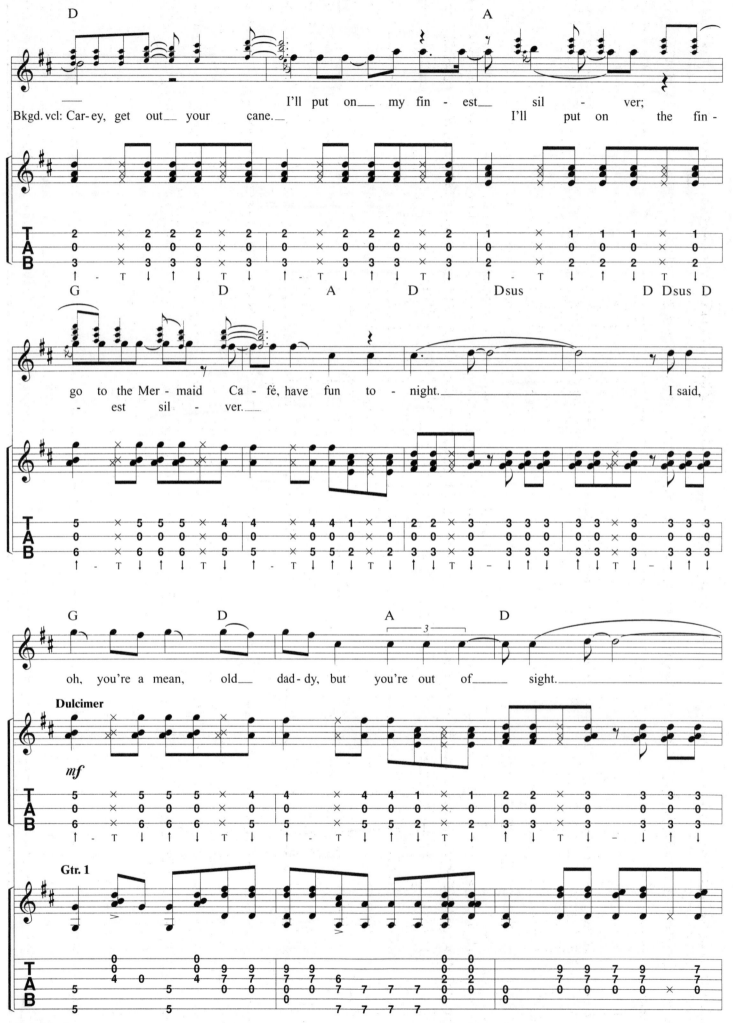

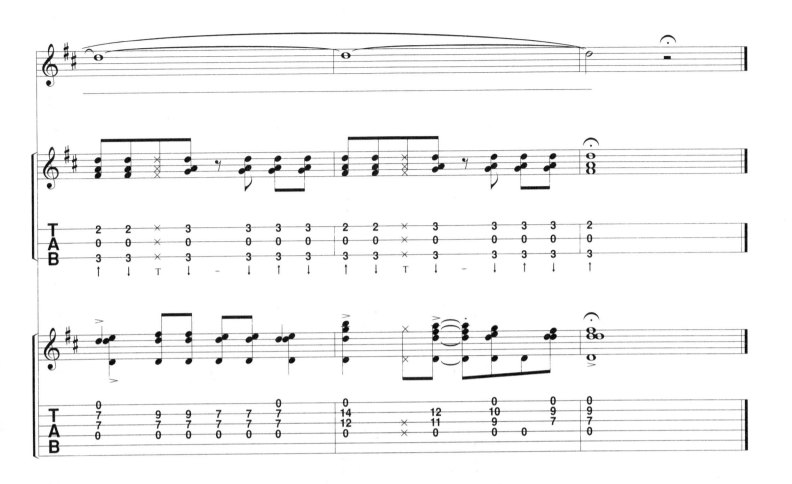

Verse 2:
Come on down to the Mermaid Café
And I will buy you a bottle of wine.
And we'll laugh and toast to nothing
And smash our empty glasses down.
Let's have a round for these freaks and these soldiers,
A round for these friends of mine.
Let's have another round for the bright red devil,
Who keeps me in this tourist town...
(To Chorus:)

Verse 3:
Maybe I'll go to Amsterdam or maybe I'll go to Rome
And rent me a grand piano and put some flowers
'Round my room.
But let's not talk about fare-thee-wells, now,
The night is a starry dome,
And they're playing that scratchy rock 'n' roll
Beneath the Matalla of the moon...
(To Chorus:)

CALIFORNIA

Words and Music by
JONI MITCHELL

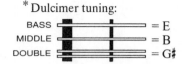

*Dulcimer tuning:

BASS = E
MIDDLE = B
DOUBLE = G♯

Gtr. 1 capo 2nd fret.

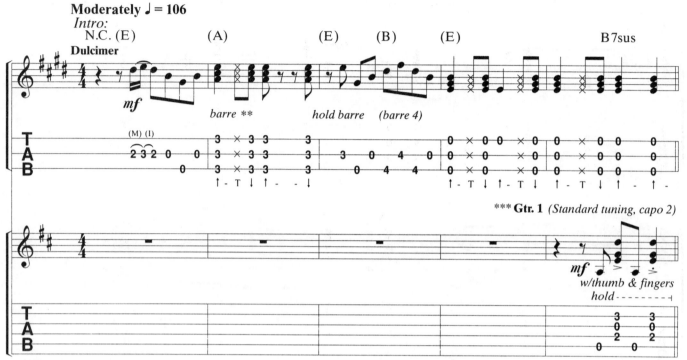

*This song is transcribed as Joni played it, in the key of E with the dulcimer tuned to EBG♯. This tuning will break most dulcimer player's strings because it is higher than dulcimers are commonly tuned. Although we have written the song out in E, we strongly suggest you play it in the key of D. Tune your dulcimer to DAF♯. It will sound just as good and you'll save your strings.
** *Barre* indicates a technique of playing all 3 strings with one finger, either your middle or index finger. (Some dulcimer players will prefer to play the barre with 3 different fingers: index on the bass string, middle on the middle and ring finger on the double/melody.) In the 3rd measure, using the barre makes it easier to pick out the melody line of the dulcimer intro.
*** Gtr. 1 is played in the key of D with a capo at the 2nd fret so that it sounds in the key of E.

California - 8 - 1
PG9666

That was just a dream some of us had.   Still a lot of_ lands__ to see,   but I would-n't wan-na

stay here._It's too_ old_ and   cold_   and_ set-tled in it's ways__ here._   Ah, but Cal-i-

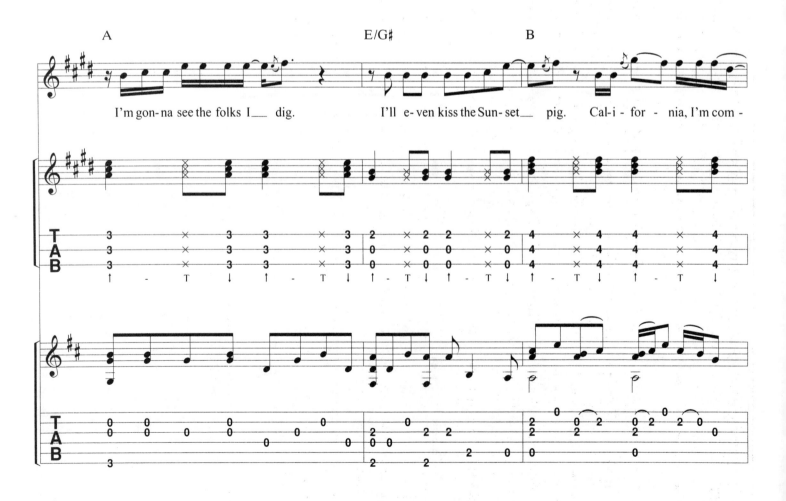

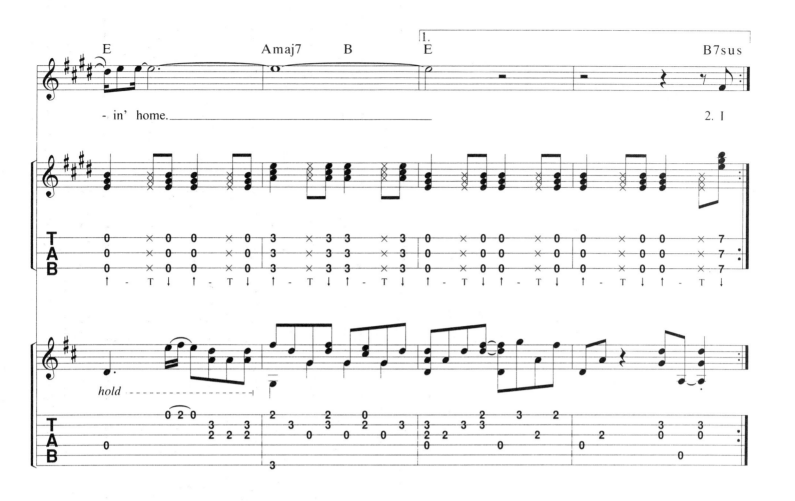

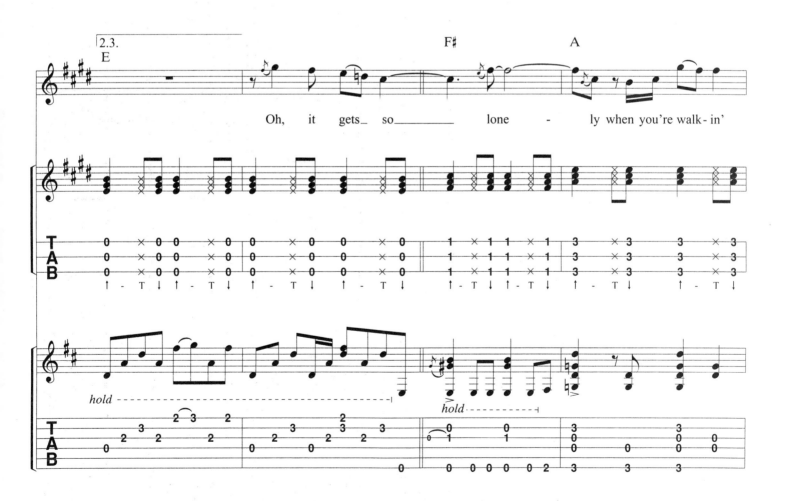

California - 8 - 4
PG9666

To Coda ⊕

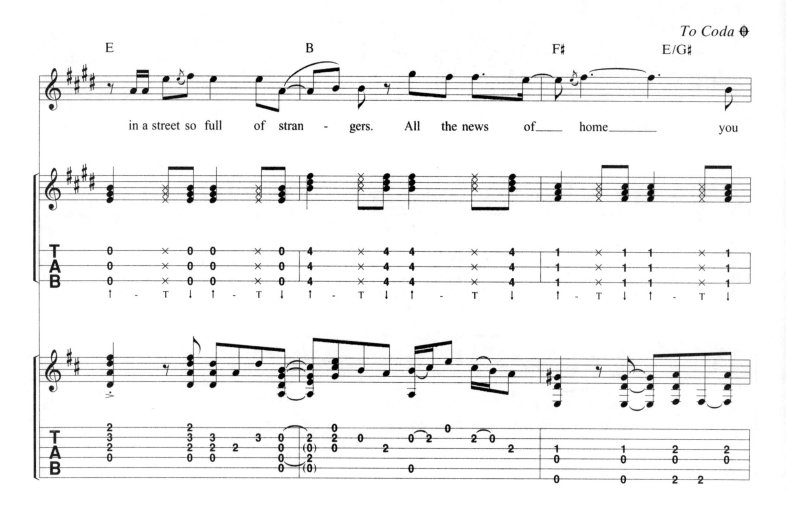

in a street so full of stran - gers. All the news of___ home_____ you

read just gives_ you_____ the blues,_____ just___ gives you

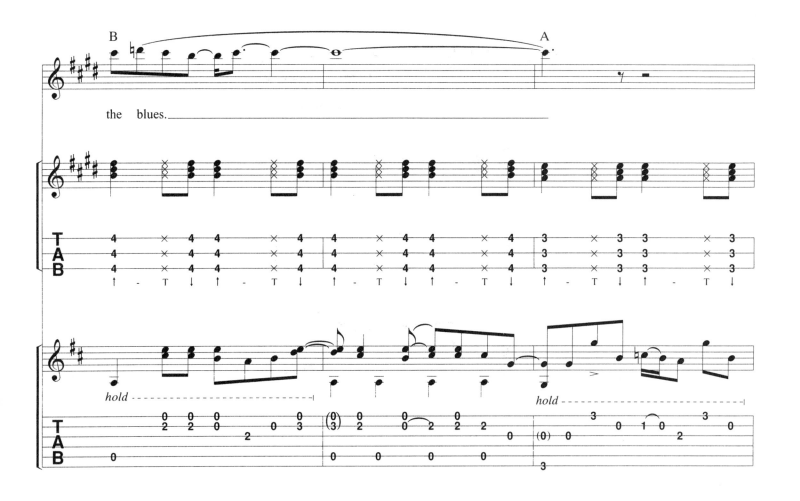

the blues._____

D.S. 𝄋 al Coda

3. So, I

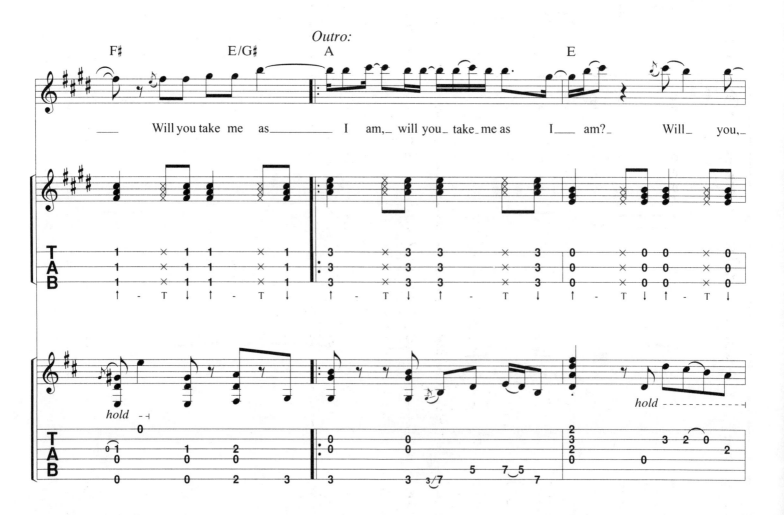

Verse 2:
I met a red-neck on a Grecian Isle, who did the "goat dance" very well.
He gave me back my smile, but he kept my camera to sell.
Oh, the rogue, the red, red rogue, he cooked good omelets and stews,
And I might have stayed on with him, but my heart cried out for you...
(To Chorus:)

Verse 3:
So, I bought me a ticket, I caught a plane to Spain.
Went to a party down a red dirt road.
There were lots of pretty people there,
Reading Rolling Stone, reading Vogue.
They said, "How long can you hang around?"
I said, "A week, maybe two,
Just until my skin turns brown and then I'm going home to California..."

YOU TURN ME ON I'M A RADIO

Words and Music by
JONI MITCHELL

Gtr. 1 tune to and Capo 1st fret:

⑥ = D ③ = F#
⑤ = A ② = A
④ = D ① = D

Moderately ♩ = 112

Intro:

D5   Dmaj7   G(9)/D

w/harmonica ad lib.

Gtr. 1 *(Acoustic, dbld.)*

mf hold throughout

*Tap muted strings w/right hand at all staccato notes.

1.
A7   A7sus

2.
A7   A7sus   D5

If you're driv-ing in-to town with a

simile

Rhy. Fig. 1

simile

Dmaj7   D   G(9)/D   D   A7   A7sus   D

dark cloud a-bove you, dial in the num-ber who's bound to love you. Oh, hon-ey,

end Rhy. Fig. 1

You Turn Me On, I'm a Radio - 7 - 1
PG9666

You Turn Me On, I'm a Radio - 7 - 2
PG9666

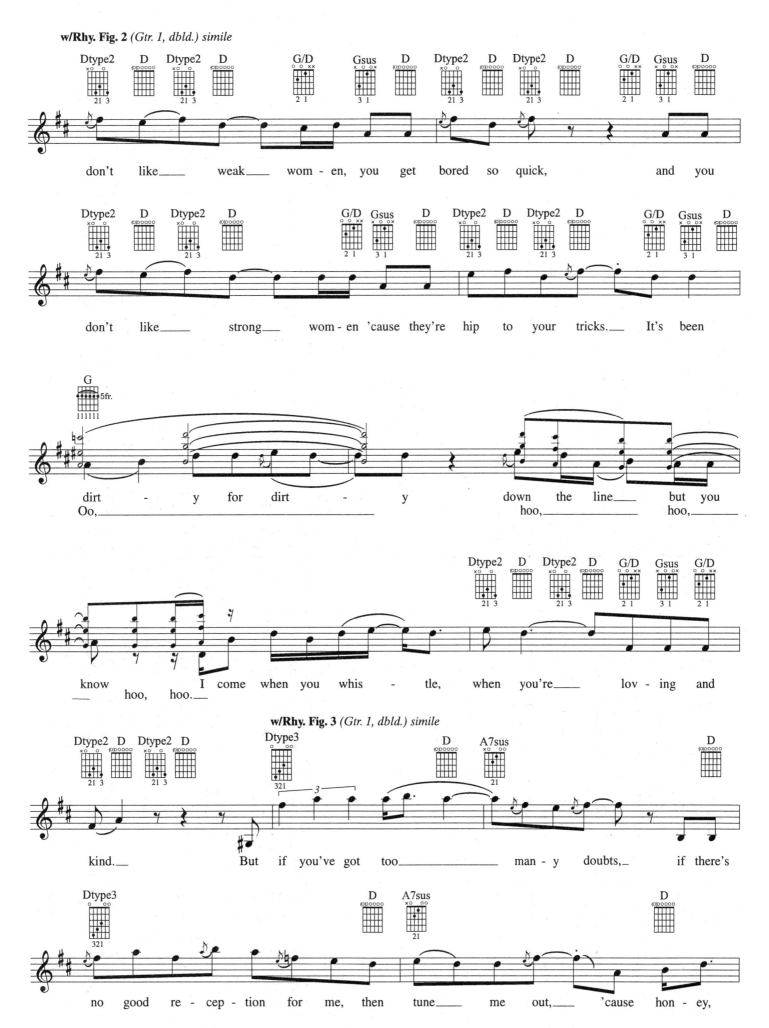

w/Rhy. Fig. 2 *(Gtr. 1, dbld.) 1st 7 bars only, simile*

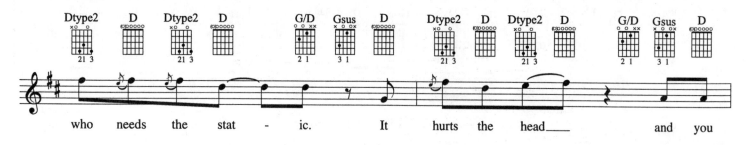

who needs the stat - ic. It hurts the head___ and you

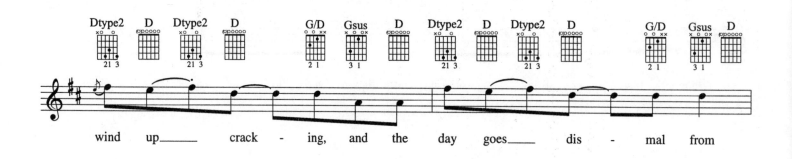

wind up___ crack - ing, and the day goes___ dis - mal from

"Break - fast Bar - ney" to the sign -

Oo,___

hoo,___ hoo,___

off prayer. What a sor - ry face___ you get to wear.___

— hoo, hoo.___ Oo,___

Gtr. 1 *(dbld.)*

I'm gon-na tell you a-gain now if you're still__ lis - t'ning there. If you're
hoo,_____ hoo,____ hoo, hoo.____

w/Rhy. **Fig. 1** *(Gtr. 1, dbld.) 5 times, simile*

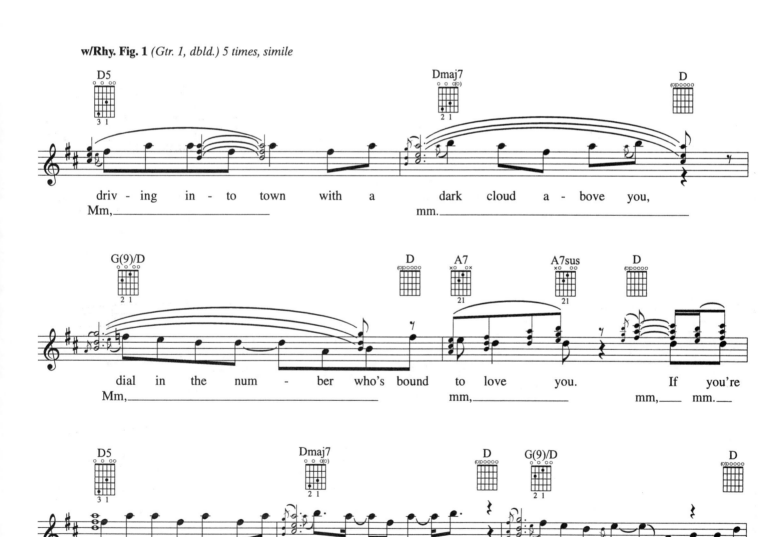

driv - ing in - to town with a dark cloud a - bove you,
Mm,_____ mm._____

dial in the num - ber who's bound to love you. If you're
Mm,_____ mm,_____ mm,___ mm.__

ly - ing on the beach with the tran - sis - tor go - ing, kick off the sand - flies, hon-ey, the
Mm, mm, mm,

You Turn Me On, I'm a Radio - 7 - 6
PG9666

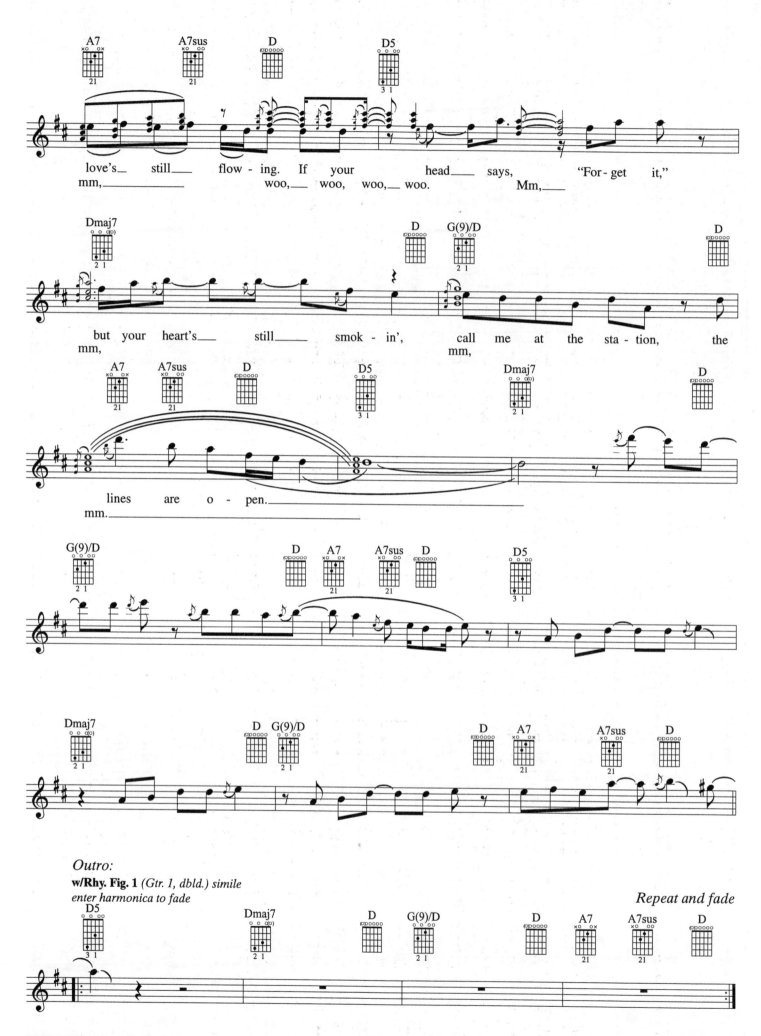

RAISED ON ROBBERY

Words and Music by
JONI MITCHELL

Gtr. 1 tune to:

⑥ = C   ③ = G
⑤ = G   ② = C
④ = C   ① = E

Moderately fast ♩ = 148

Intro:

C6

Gtr. 3 (w/wah effect)

Rhy. Fig. 1

w/Rhy. Fig. 1 *(Gtr. 3) 2 times, simile*

He was sit-tin' in the lounge of the Em-pire Ho-tel.___ He was

*Unison vocals -----

end Rhy. Fig. 1

Gtr. 2 *(Electric)*

8va------

*Dbld. by gtr. in "Nashville" tuning.
**Gtr. 3 simile ad lib. Gtr. 2.

Raised on Robbery - 9 - 2
PG9666

64

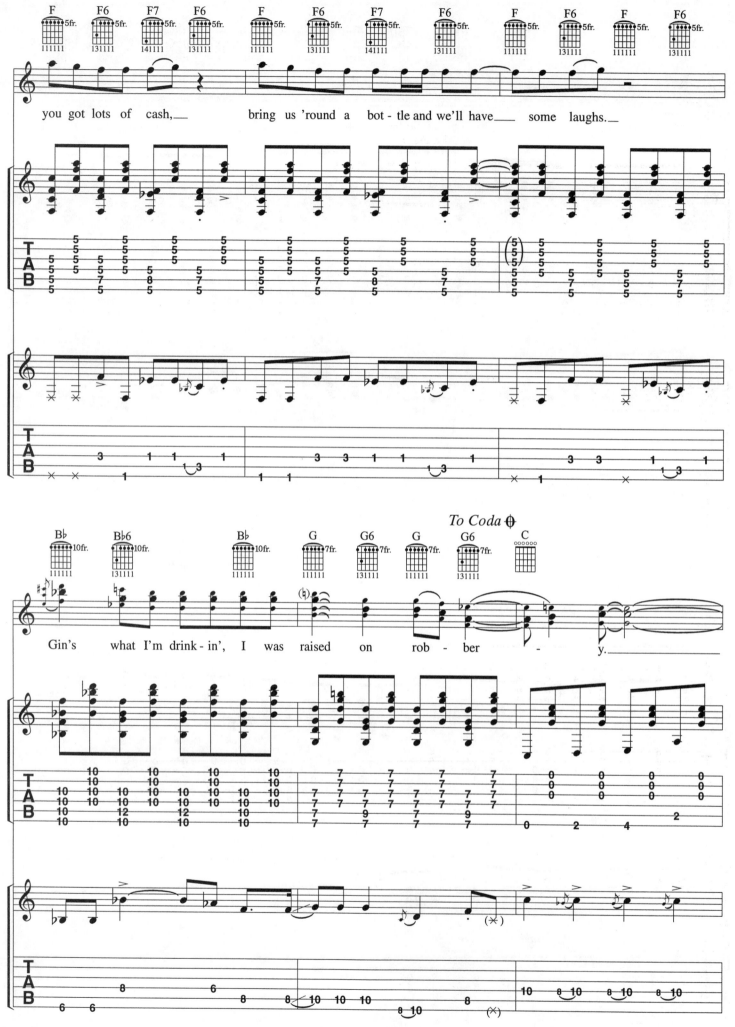

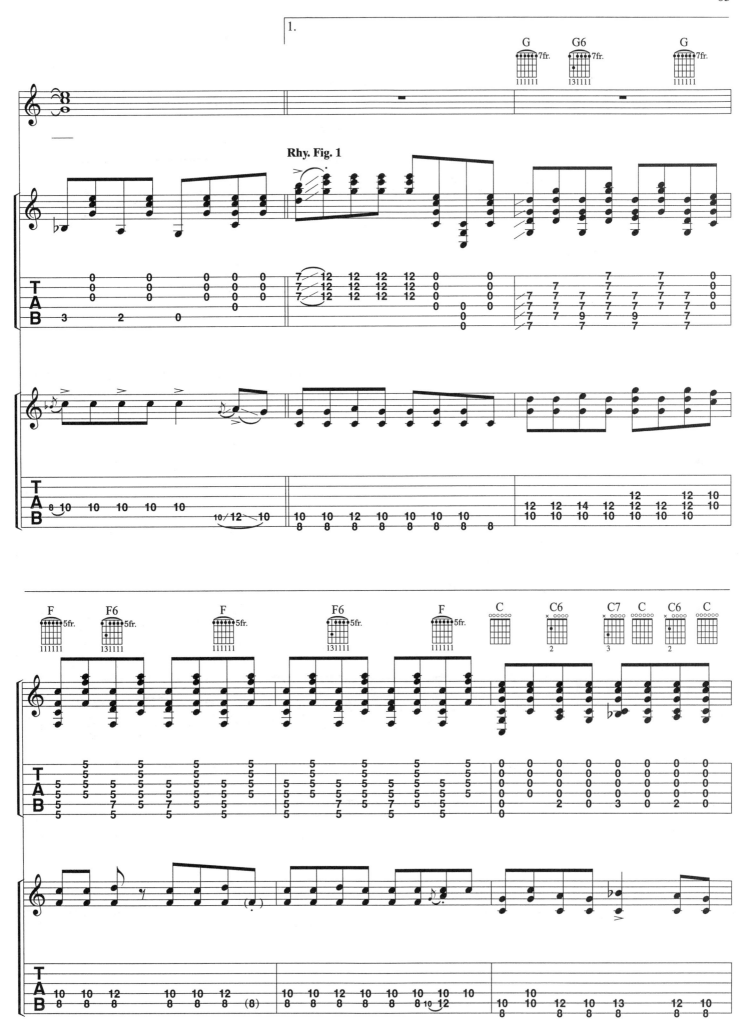

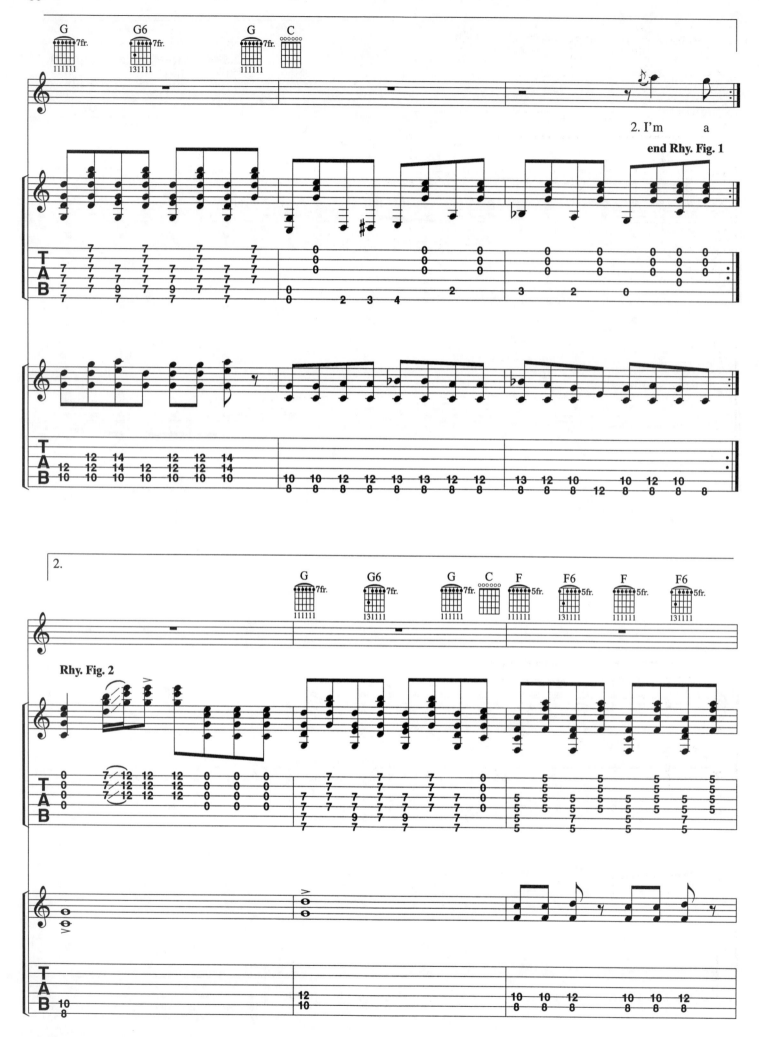

3. **w/Rhy. Fig. 1** *(Gtr. 1) simile*

3. We

end Rhy. Fig. 2

Gtr. 2

hold

hold

68

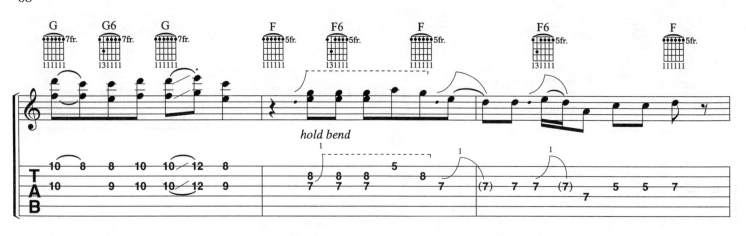

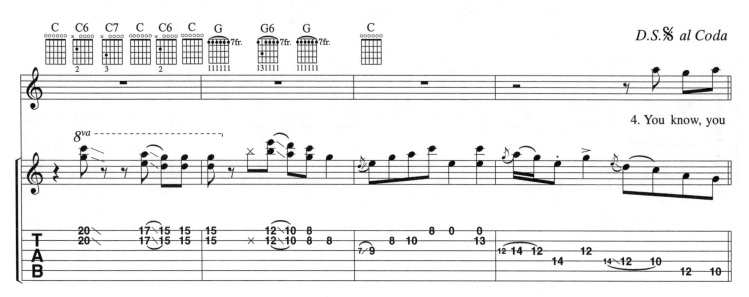

D.S. % al Coda

4. You know, you

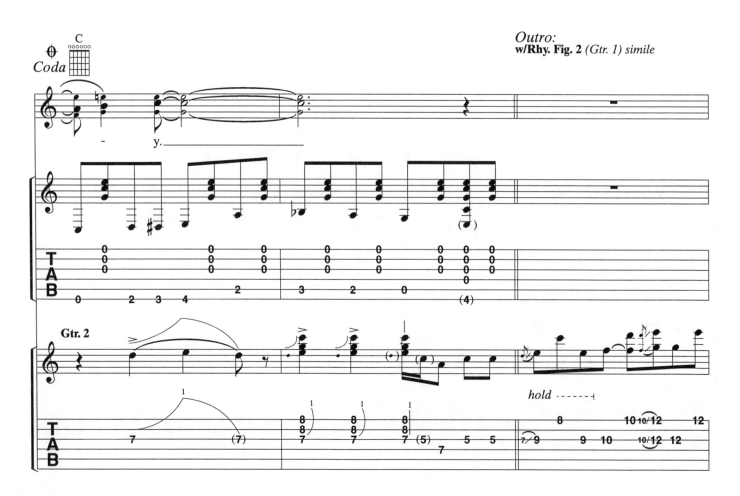

Outro:
w/Rhy. Fig. 2 *(Gtr. 1) simile*

Raised on Robbery - 9 - 8
PG9666

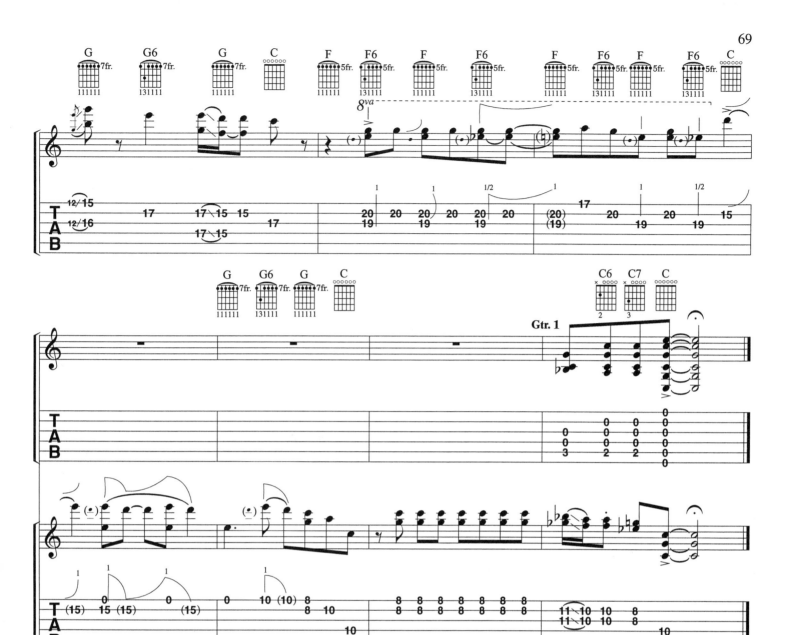

Verse 2:
I'm a pretty good cook, I'm sitting on my groceries.
Come up to my kitchen, I'll show you my best recipes.
I try and I try, but I can't save a cent.
I'm up after midnight cooking,
Trying to make my rent.
I'm rough but I'm pleasing,
I was raised on robbery.

Verse 3:
We had a little money once,
They were pushing through a four-lane highway.
Government gave us three thousand dollars.
You should've seen it fly away.
First he bought a '57 Biscayne,
He put it in the ditch.
He drunk up all the rest, that son of a bitch.
His blood's bad whiskey,
I was raised on robbery.

Verse 4:
You know, you ain't bad looking.
I like the way you hold your drinks.
Come home with me, honey,
I ain't asking for no full-length mink.
Hey, where you going?
Don't go yet, your glass ain't empty and we just met.
You're mean when you're loaded,
I was raised on robbery.

HELP ME

Gtr. 1 tune to:
⑥ = C   ③ = E
⑤ = G   ② = B
④ = E   ① = E

Words and Music by
JONI MITCHELL

Moderately fast ♩ = 172

Intro:

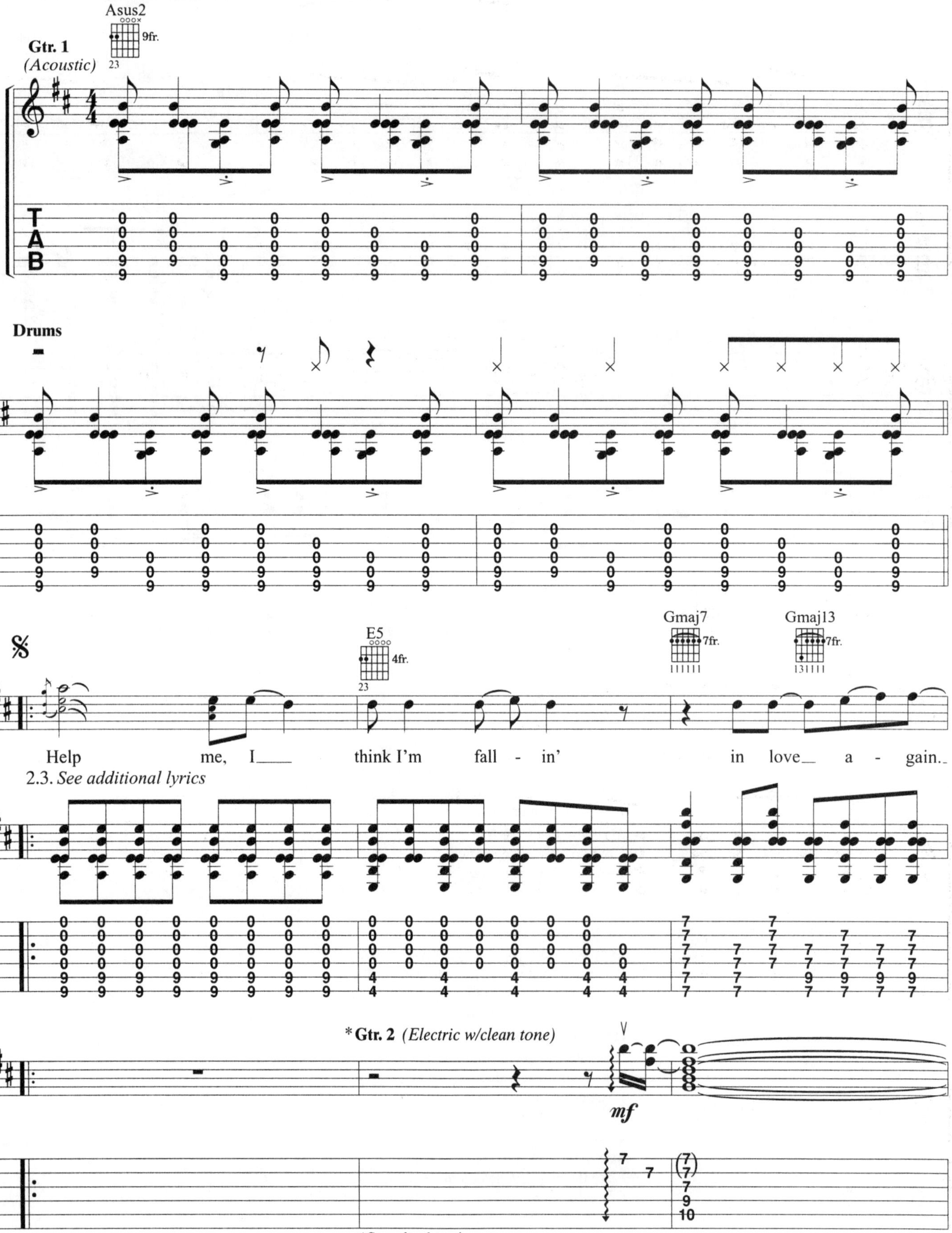

2.3. See additional lyrics

Help me, I___ think I'm fall - in' in love___ a - gain.___

*Gtr. 2 (Electric w/clean tone)

mf

*Standard tuning.

Help Me - 10 - 1
PG9666

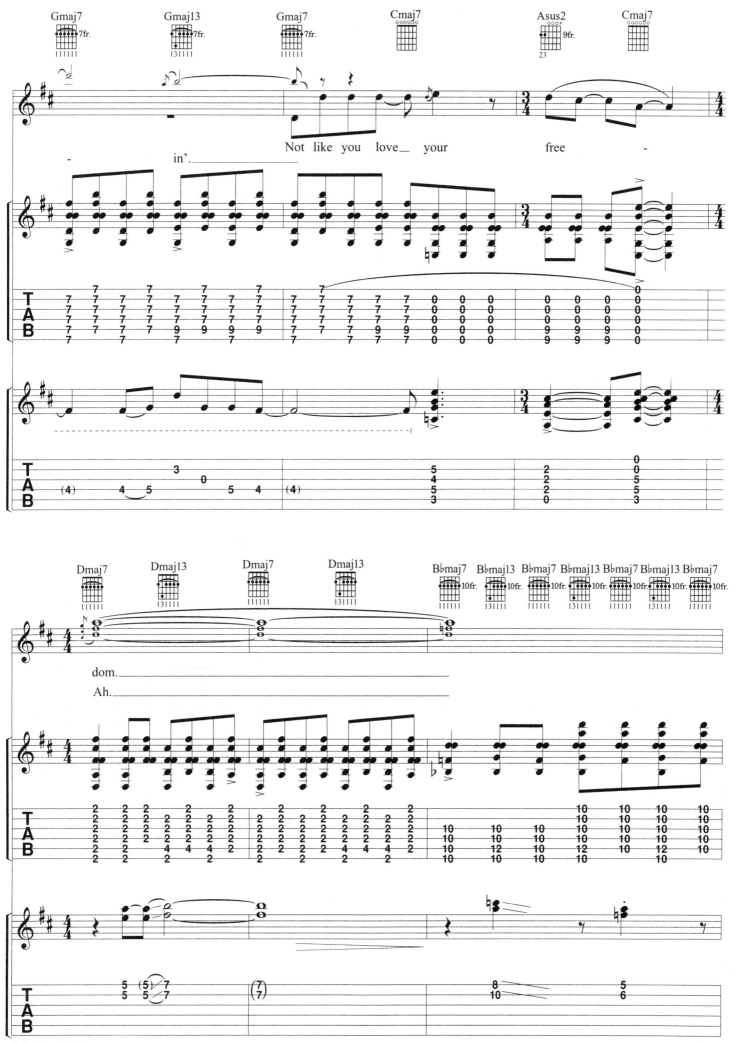

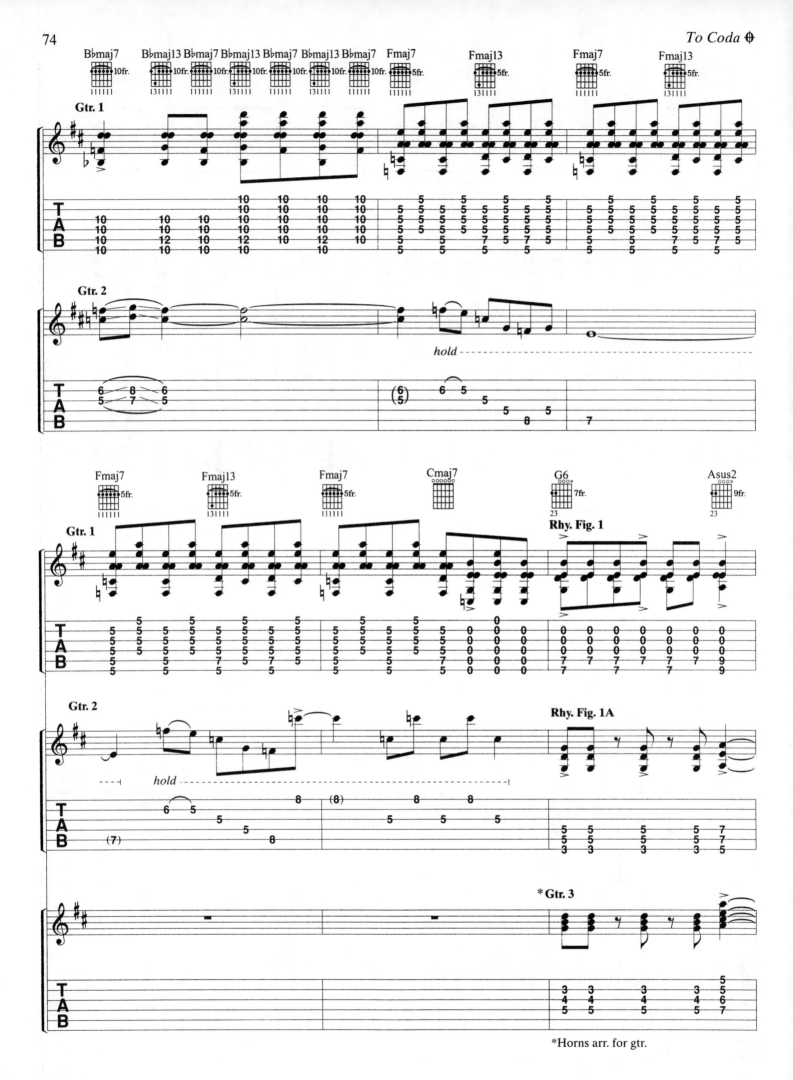

*Horns arr. for gtr.

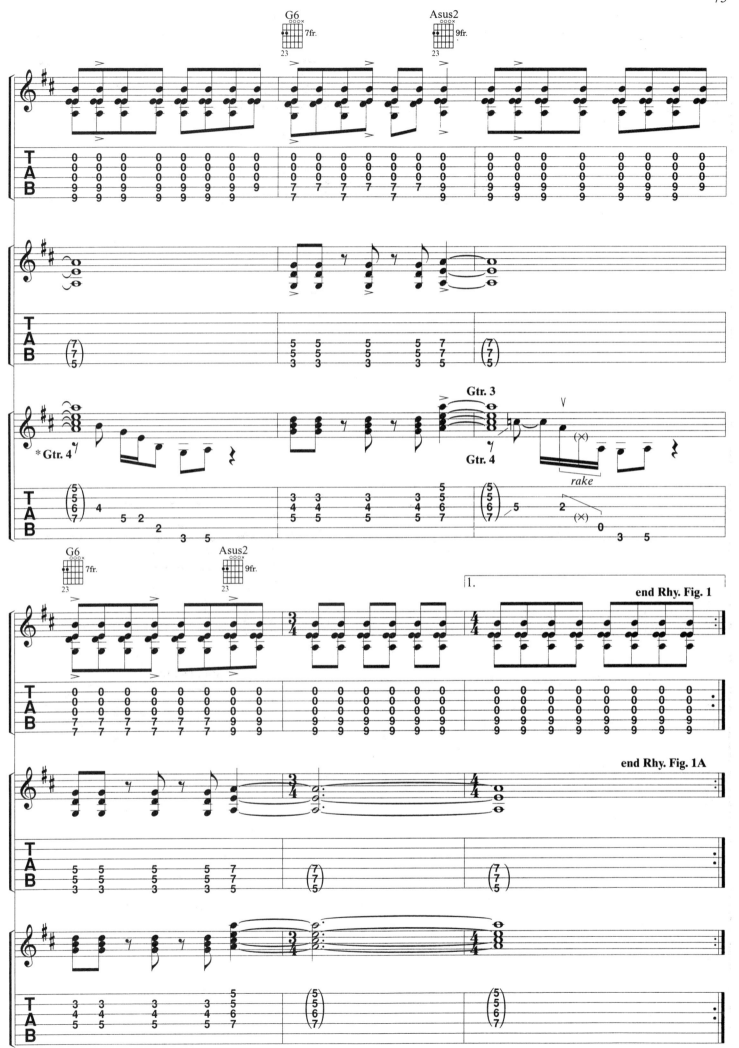

*Horns arr. for gtr.

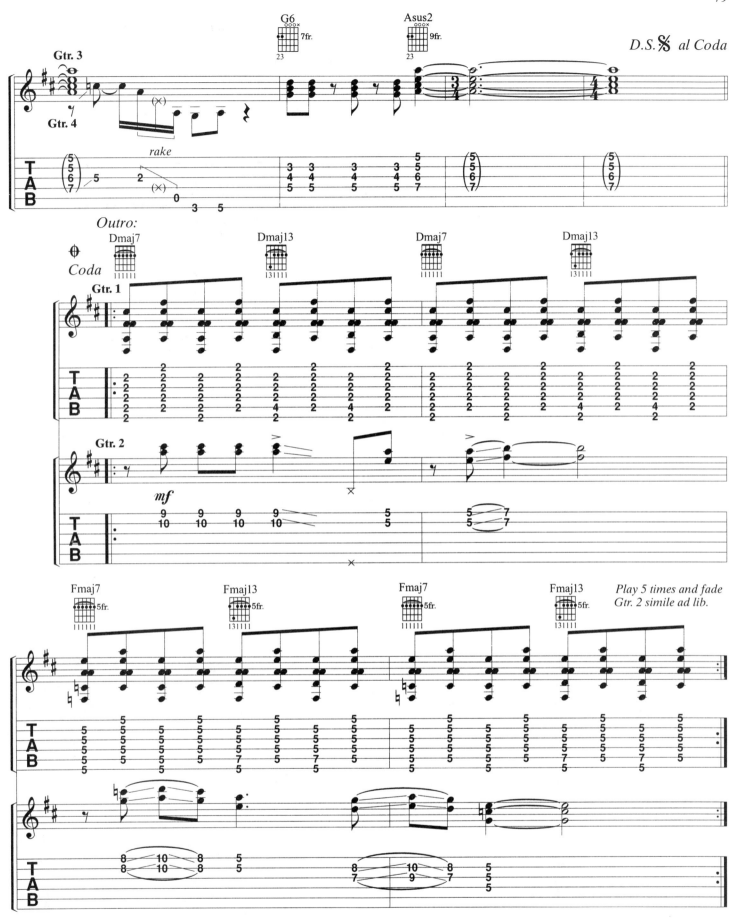

Verse 2:

Help me, I think I'm fallin' in love too fast.
It's got me hoping for the future
And worrying about the past.
'Cause I've seen some hot, hot blazes
Come down to smoke and ash.
We love our lovin',
But not like we love our freedom.

Verse 3:

Help me, I think I'm fallin' in love with you.
Are you gonna let me go there by myself?
That's such a lonely thing to do,
Both of us flirting around,
Flirting and flirtin', hurtin', too.
We love our lovin',
But not like we love our freedom.

FREE MAN IN PARIS

Words and Music by
JONI MITCHELL

Gtr. 1 tune to:
⑥ = D   ③ = G
⑤ = A   ② = B
④ = D   ① = D

Moderately fast ♩ = 164
Intro:

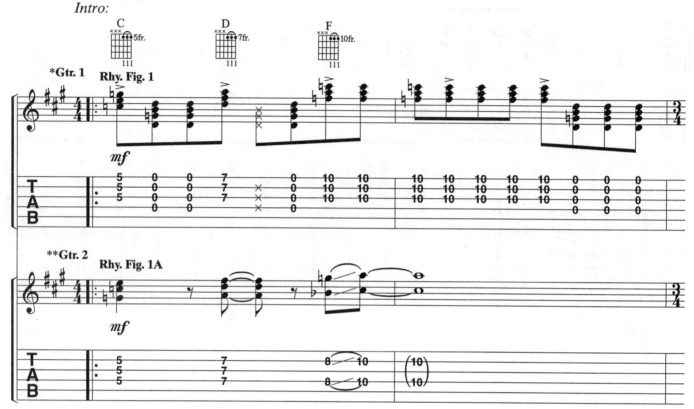

*Two gtrs. arranged for one.
**Gtrs. 2 & 3 tacet first time.

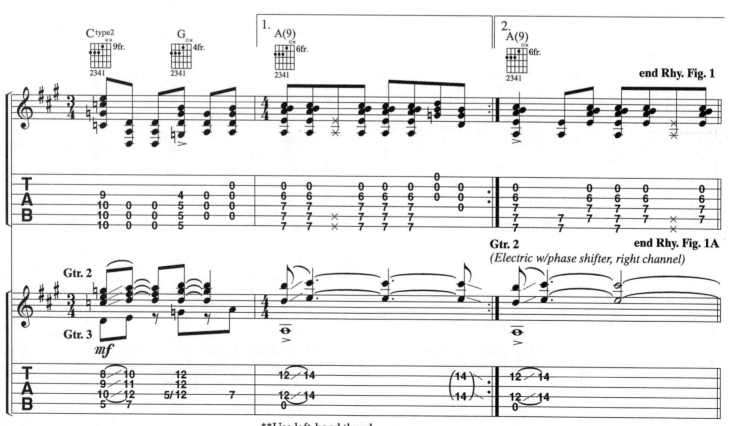

**Use left-hand thumb.

Free Man in Paris - 11 - 1
PG9666

1. "The way___ I

𝄋 *Verses:*

see it," he___ said, "you just can't win it.___
2. *See additional lyrics*

Rhy. Fig. 2

hold throughout

*Gtrs. 2 & 3

hold -

*Two gtrs. arranged for one.

Free Man in Paris - 11 - 2
PG9666

*Use left-hand thumb.

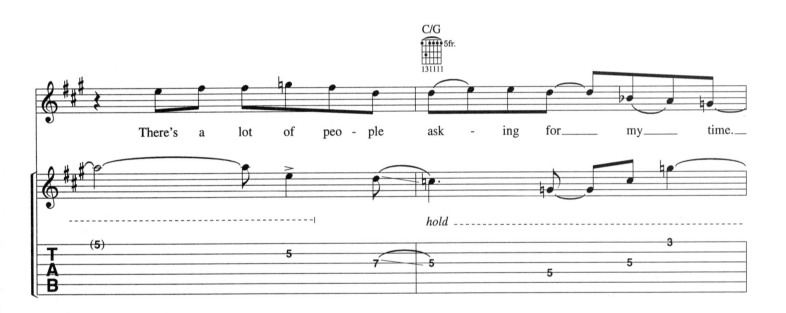

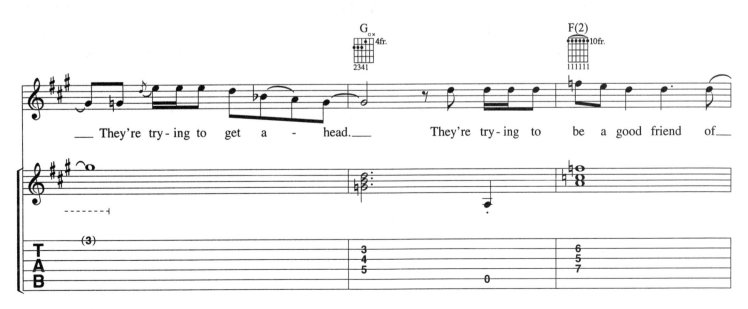

Chorus:

I was a free man in Par - is, I felt un -

*Gtrs. 2 & 3

*Two gtrs. arranged for one.

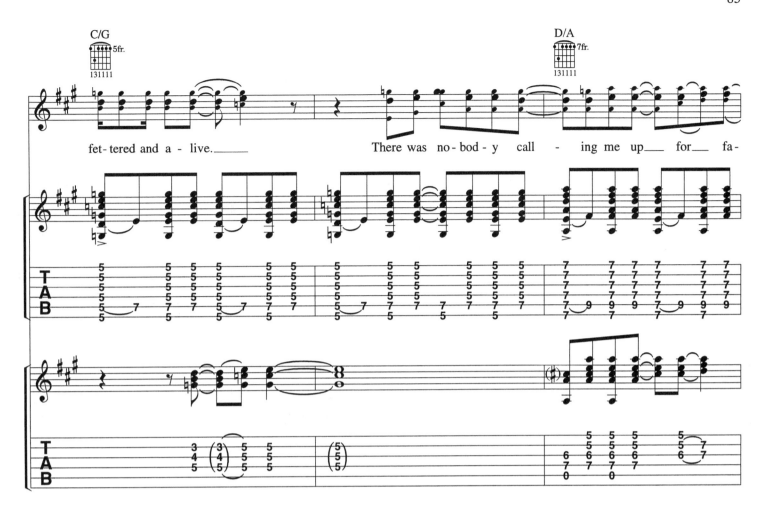

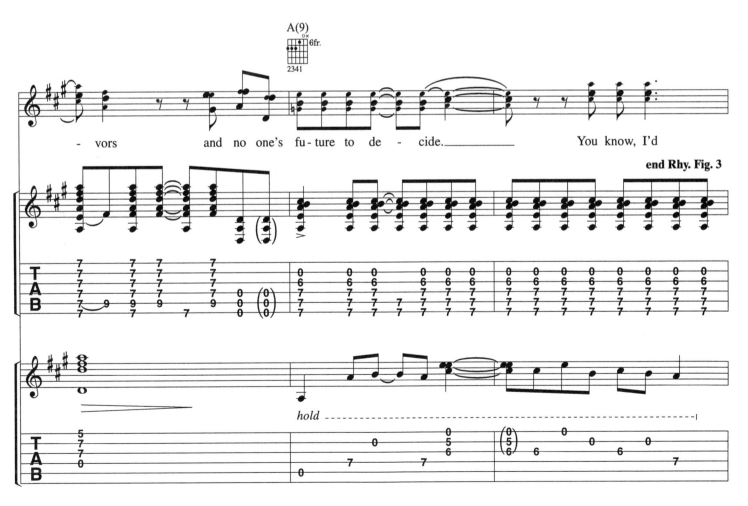

Free Man in Paris - 11 - 6
PG9666

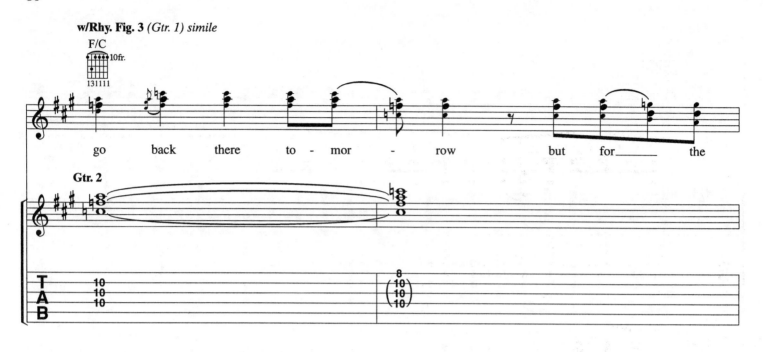

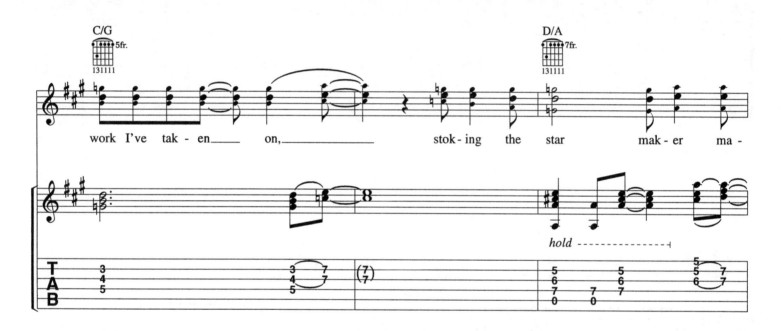

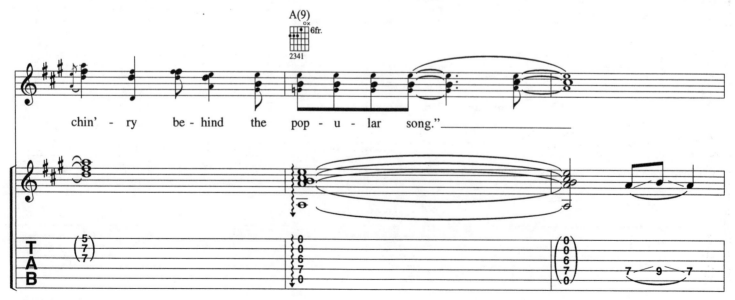

Interlude:

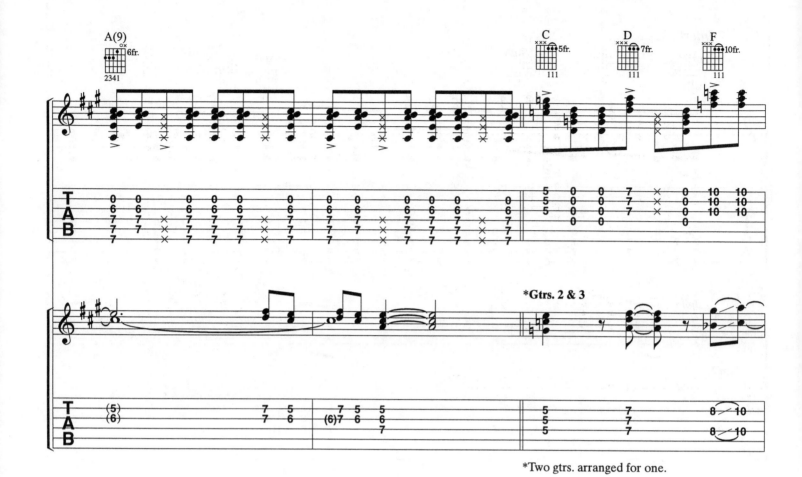

*Two gtrs. arranged for one.

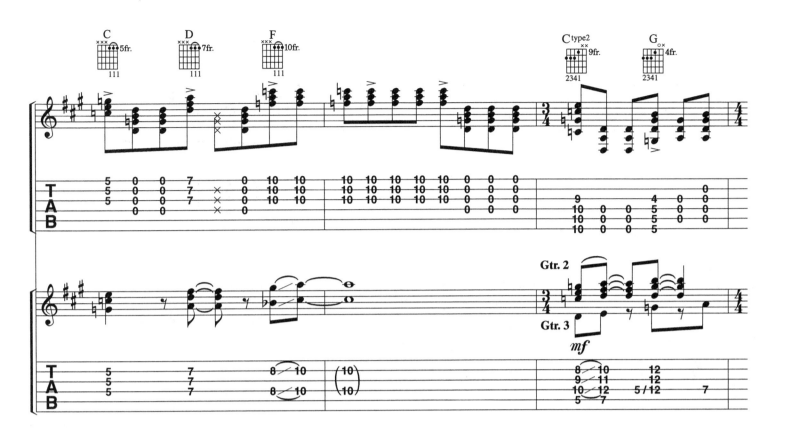

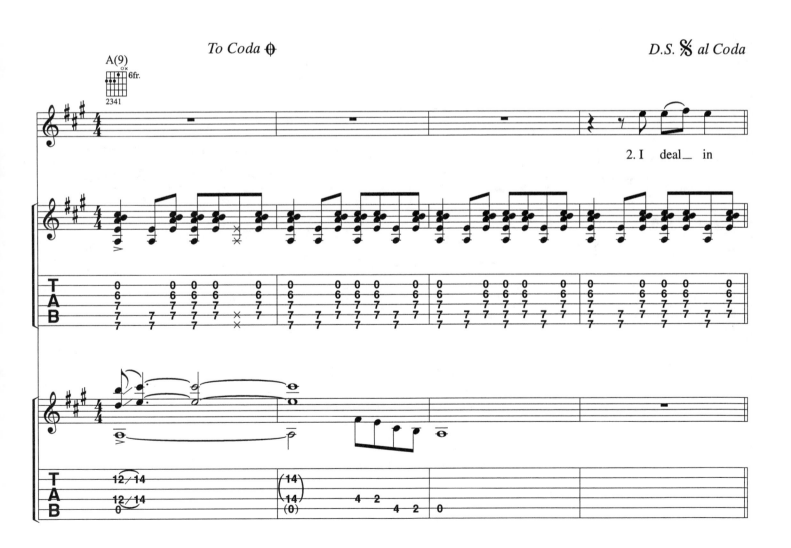

90

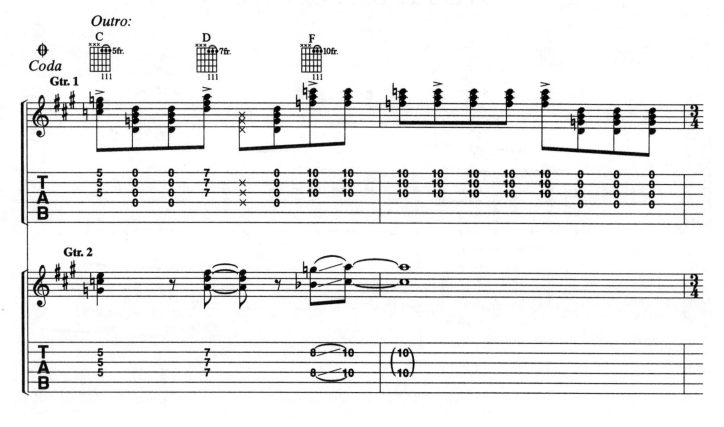

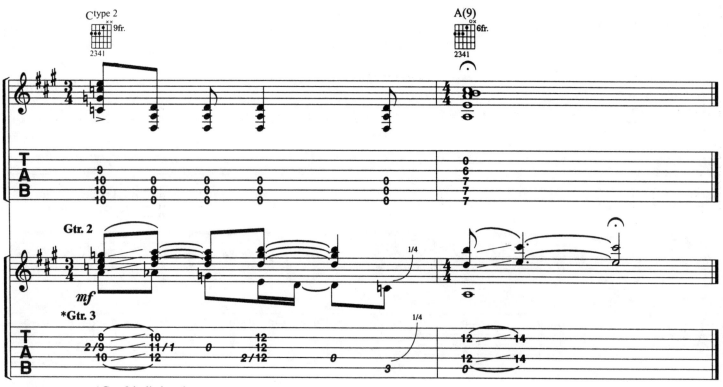

*Gtr. 3 italic in tab.

Verse 2:
I deal in dreamers and telephone screamers.
Lately, I wonder what I do it for.
If I had my way, I'd just
Walk through those doors and wander
Down the Champs Élysees,
Going café to cabaret,
Thinking how I'll feel when I find
That very good friend of mine.

Free Man in Paris - 11 - 11
PG9666

BOTH SIDES, NOW

Words and Music by
JONI MITCHELL

Gtr. 1 Capo 2; tuning:

⑥ = E ③ = G#

⑤ = B ② = B

④ = E ① = E

Moderately ♩ = 98

Intro:

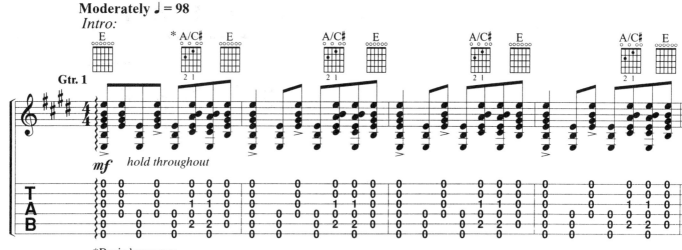

*Basic harmony.

Verses:

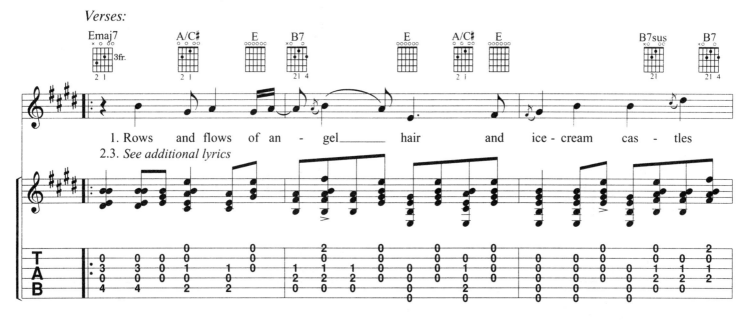

1. Rows and flows of an - gel_____ hair and ice - cream cas - tles
2.3. *See additional lyrics*

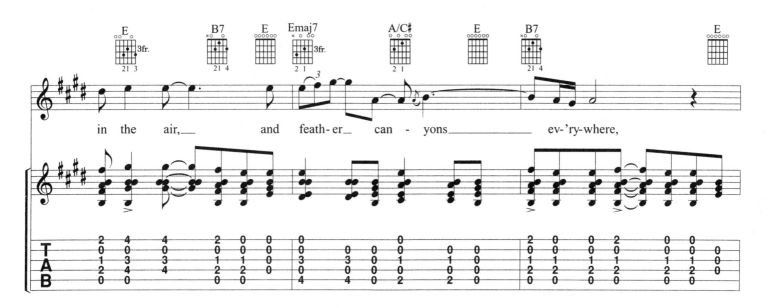

in the air,___ and feath - er__ can - yons_____ ev - 'ry - where,

Both Sides, Now - 5 - 1
PG9666

92

Both Sides, Now - 5 - 2
PG9666

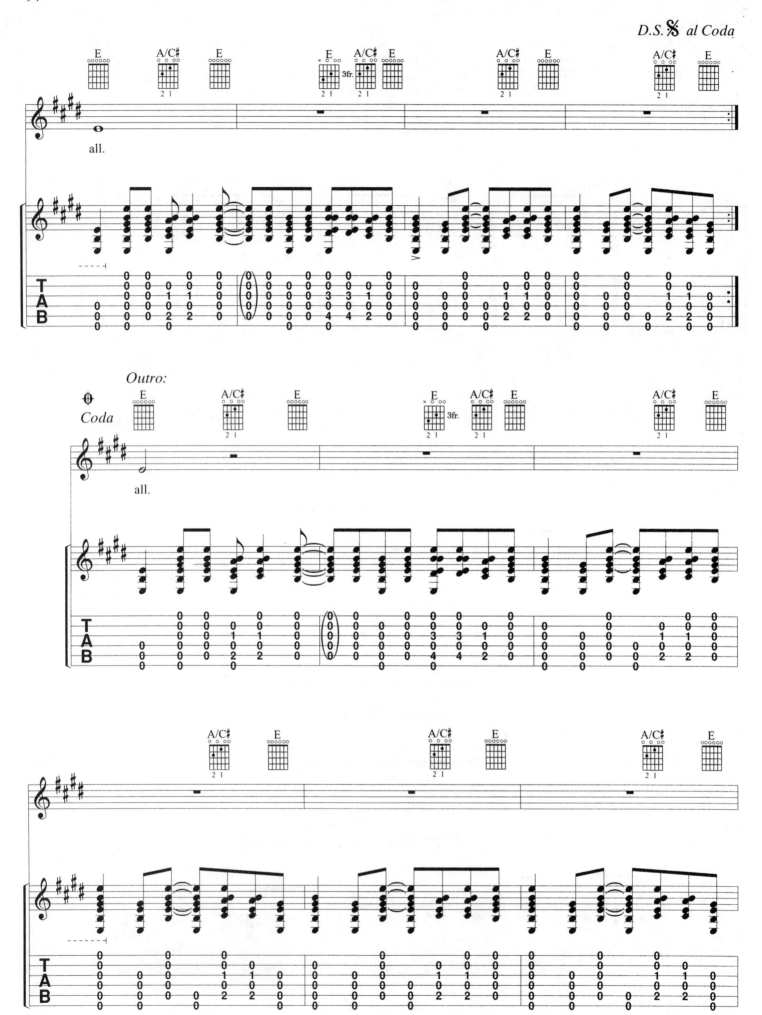

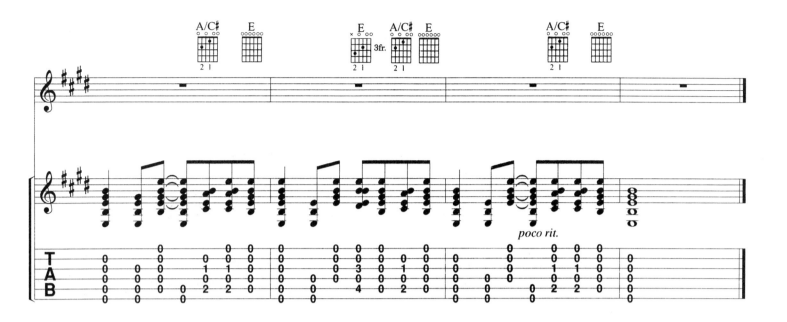

poco rit.

Verse 2:
Moons and Junes and Ferris wheels,
The dizzy dancing way you feel,
As every fairy tale comes real,
I've looked at love that way.
But now it's just another show,
You leave 'em laughing when you go.
And if you care, don't let them know,
Don't give yourself away.

Chorus 2:
I've looked at love from both sides now,
From give and take, and still, somehow
It's love's illusions I recall.
I really don't know love at all.

Verse 3:
Tears and fears and feeling proud,
To say "I love you" right out loud,
Dreams and schemes and circus crowds,
I've look at life that way.
But now old friends are acting strange,
They shake their heads, they say I've changed.
Well, something's lost but something's gained,
In living every day.

Chorus 3:
I've looked at life from both sides now,
From win and lose, and still, somehow
It's life's illusions I recall.
I really don't know life at all.

RIVER

Words and Music by
JONI MITCHELL

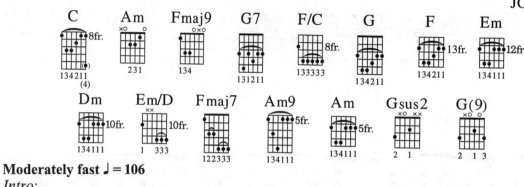

Moderately fast ♩ = 106

Intro:

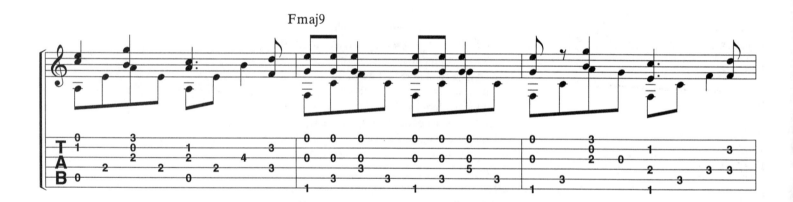

Piano arranged for guitar.

𝄋 *Verses 1 & 3:*

1. 3. It's com-ing on Christ-mas,__ they're

River - 8 - 1
PG9666

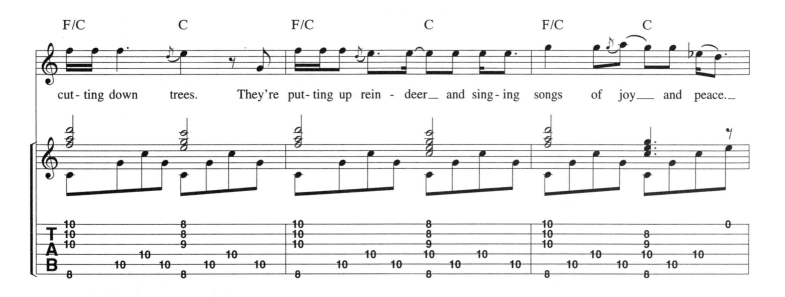

cut-ting down trees. They're put-ting up rein - deer_ and sing-ing songs of joy_ and peace._

To Coda ⊕

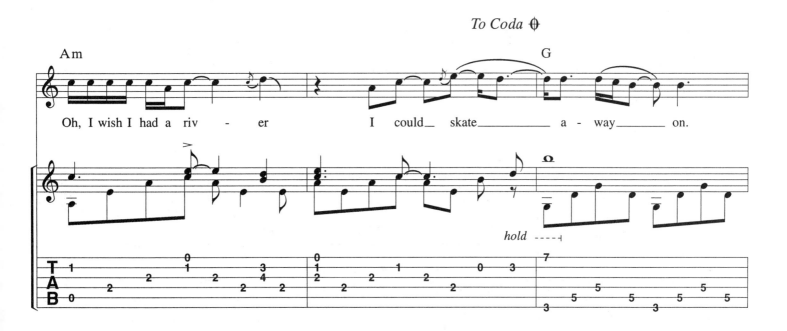

Oh, I wish I had a riv - er I could_ skate_____ a - way_____ on.

hold ----

w/Rhy. Fig. 1 *(Gtr. 1) 1st 6 measures, simile*

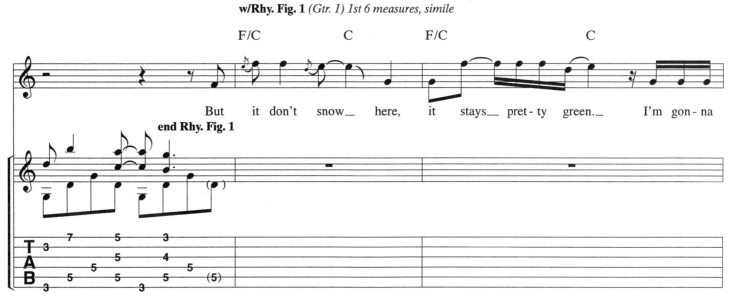

But it don't snow_ here, it stays_ pret-ty green._ I'm gon-na

end Rhy. Fig. 1

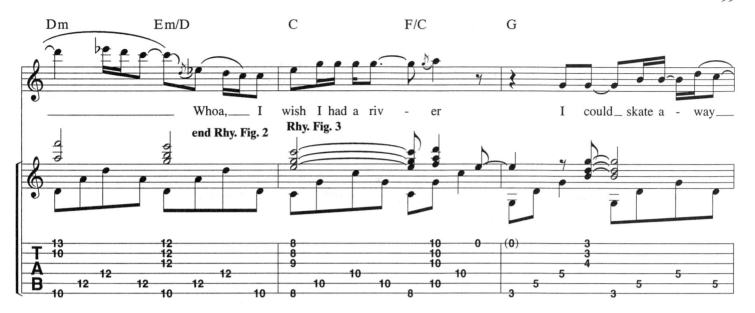

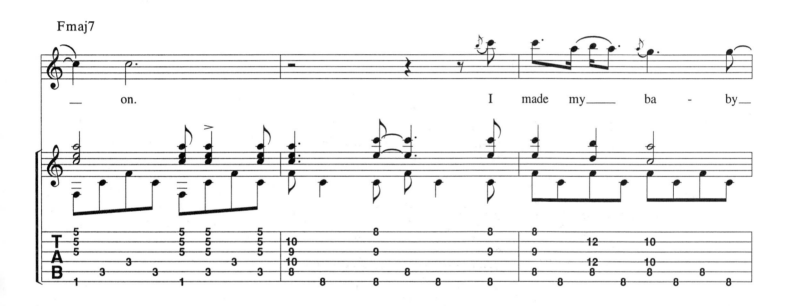

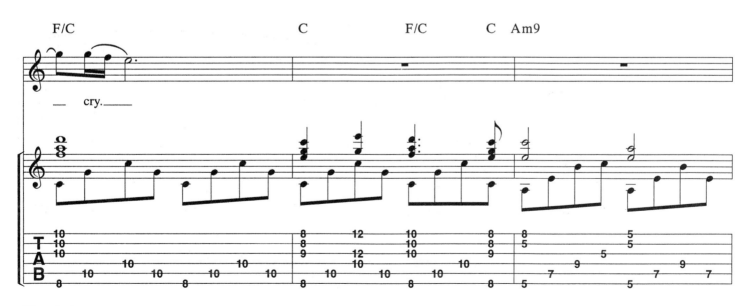

River - 8 - 4

PG9666

He tried___
end Rhy. Fig. 3

Verse 2:
w/Rhy. Fig. 1 *(Gtr. 1) simile*

___ hard___ to help___ me, you know. He put me at___ ease_____ and he

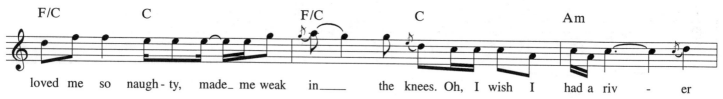

loved me so naugh-ty, made_ me weak in___ the knees. Oh, I wish I had a riv - er

I could_ skate_____ a - way_____ on. I'm so hard to han - dle, I'm

sel - fish and I'm sad. Now I've gone and lost the best_ ba - by that I_____

___ ev - er___ had. Oh, I wish_ I had a riv - er I could_ skate_____

River - 8 - 5
PG9666

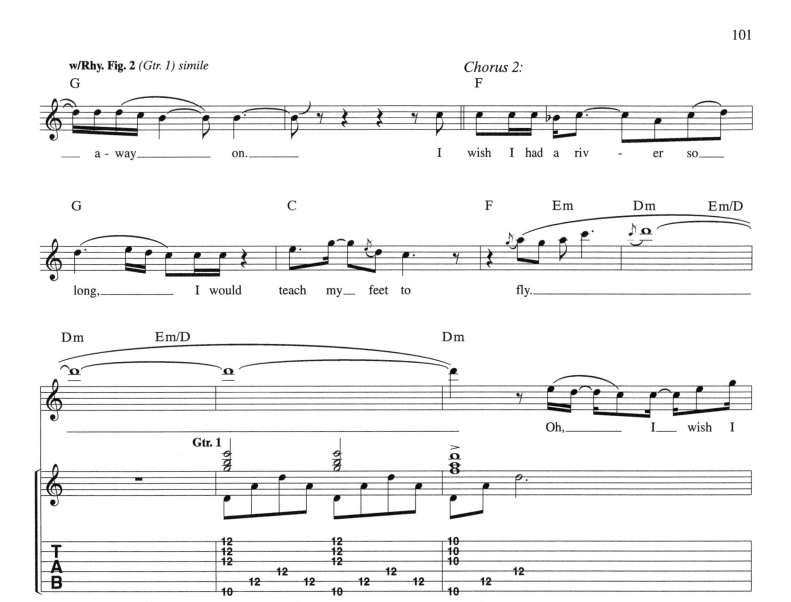

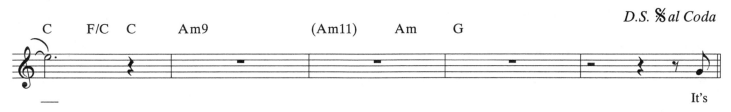

River - 8 - 6
PG9666

Coda

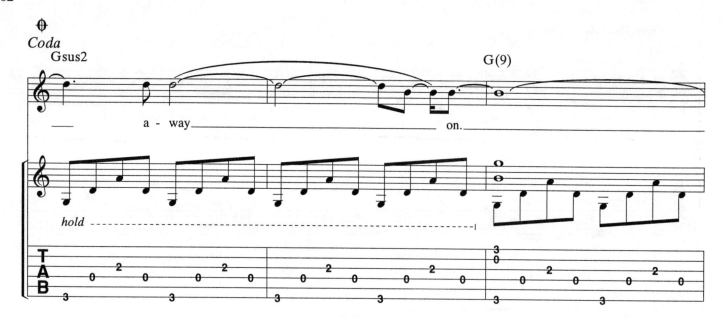

Outro:

Fmaj7   F

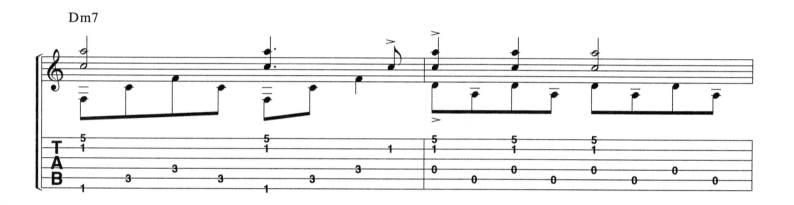

Dm7

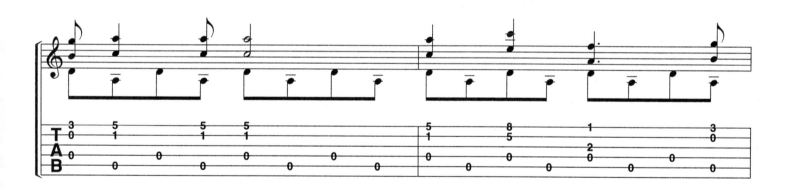

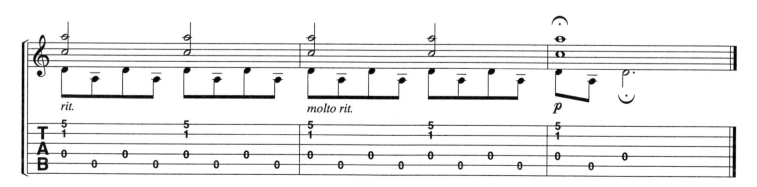

rit.   molto rit.   p

CHINESE CAFE/UNCHAINED MELODY

Words and Music by
JONI MITCHELL/
Words by HY ZARET,
Music by ALEX NORTH

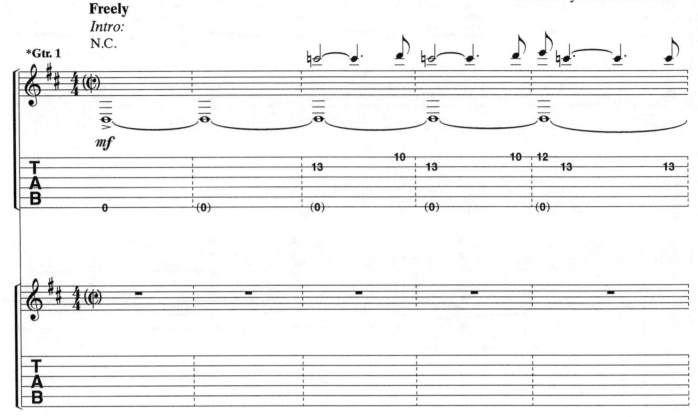

*Keybd./synth./bass-composite arrangement for gtr.
Tune ⑥ string down to D.

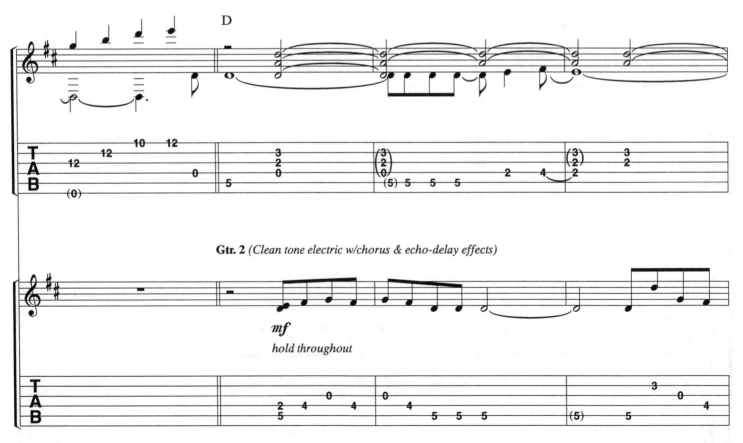

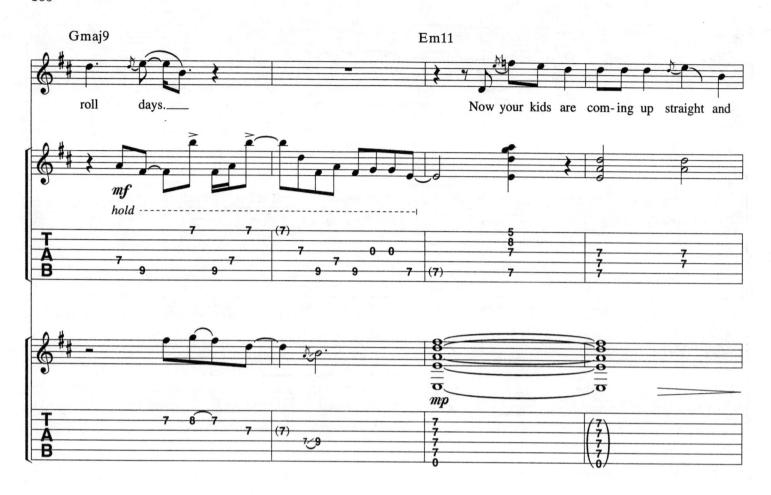

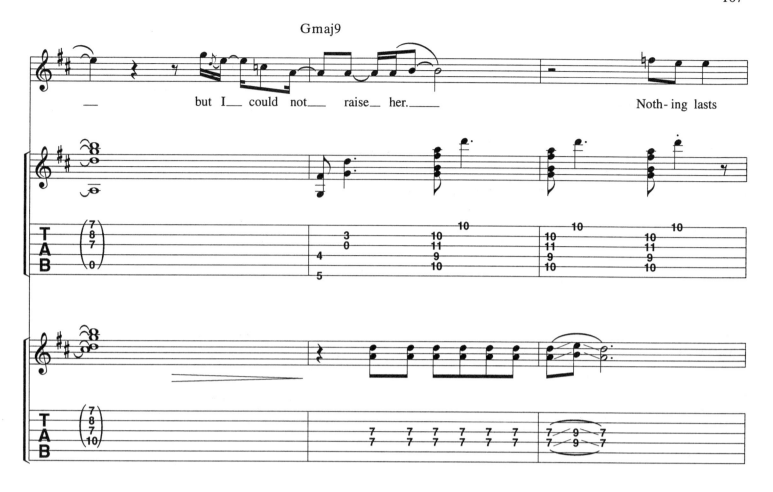

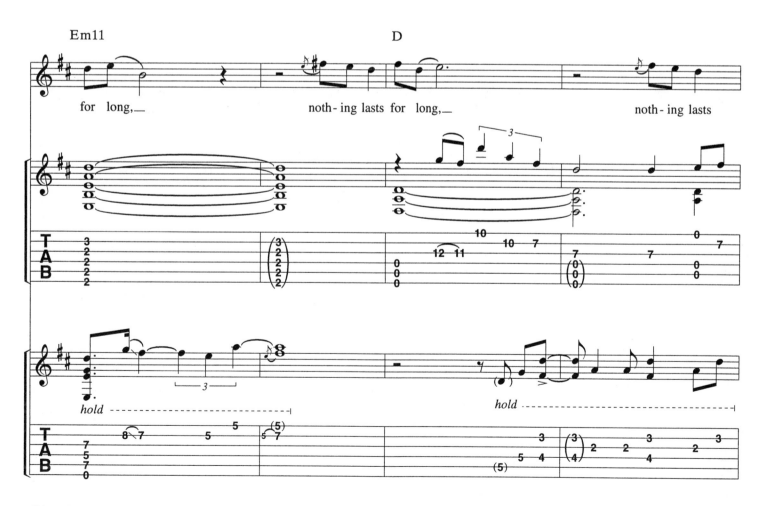

Chinese Cafe - 12 - 4

PG9666

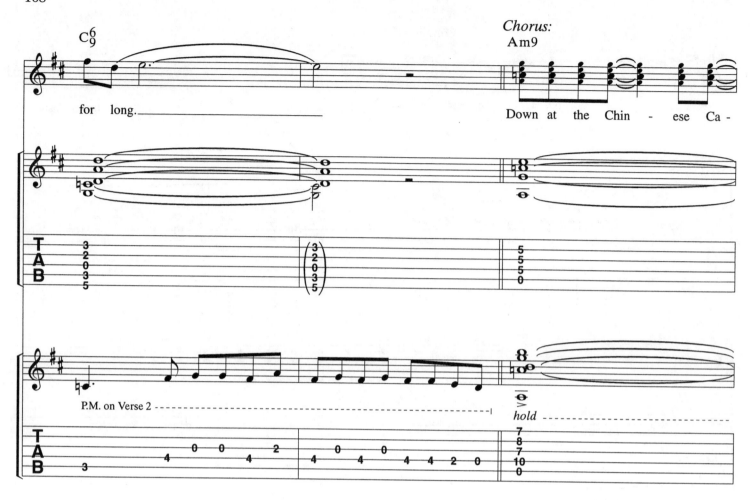

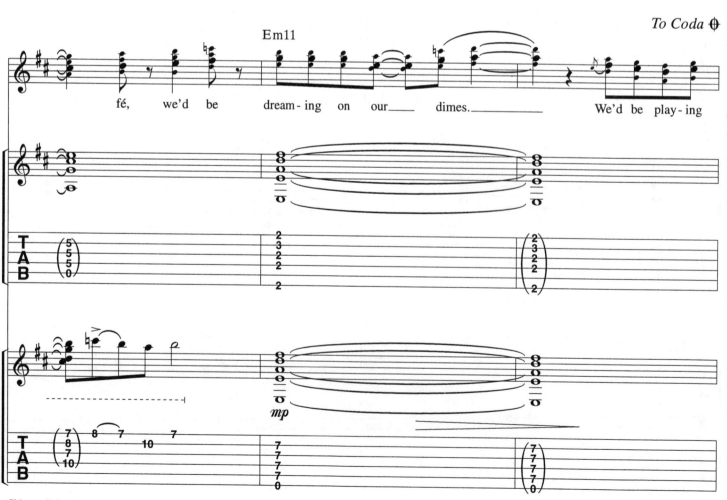

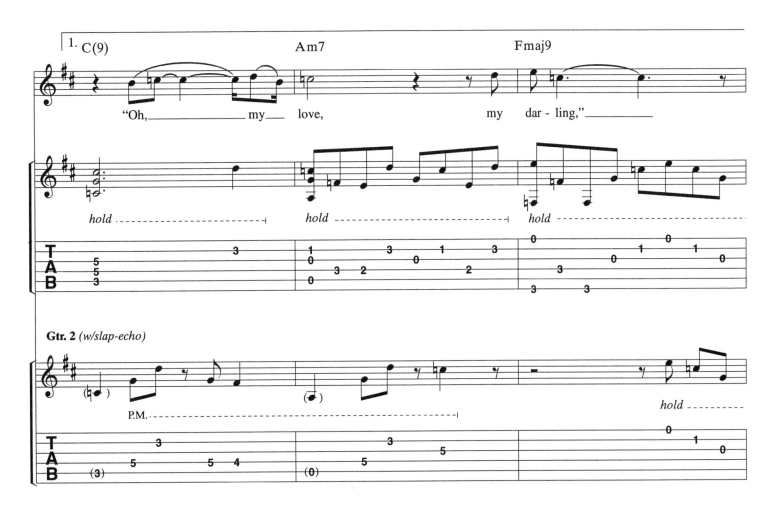

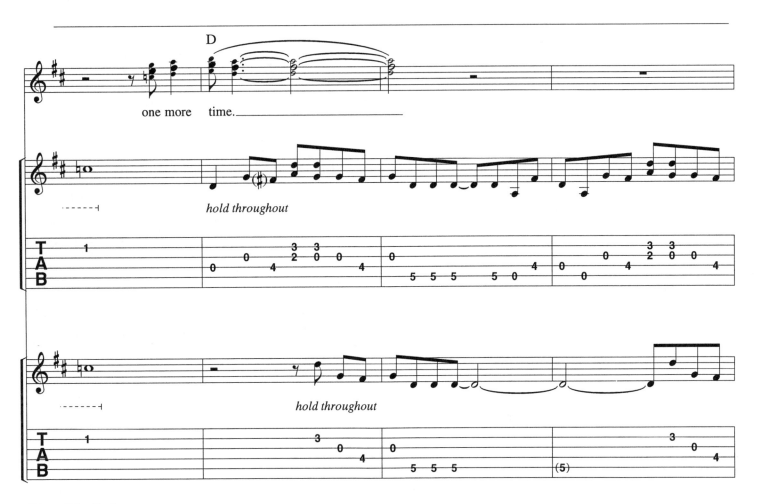

Chinese Cafe - 12 - 6
PG9666

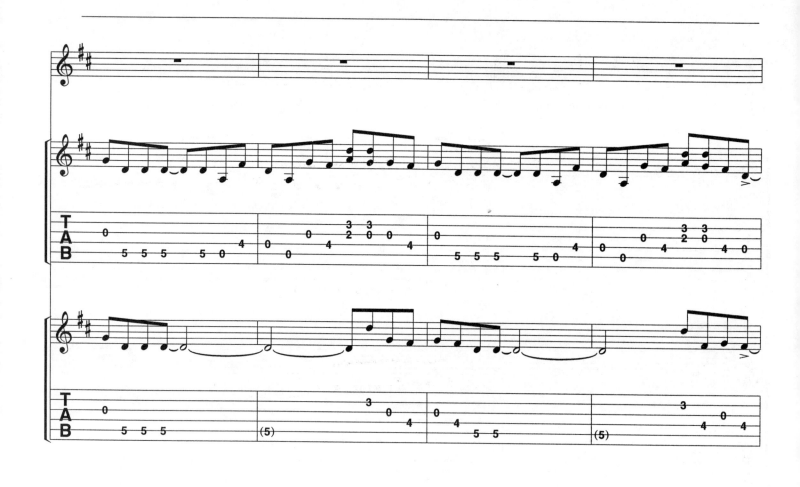

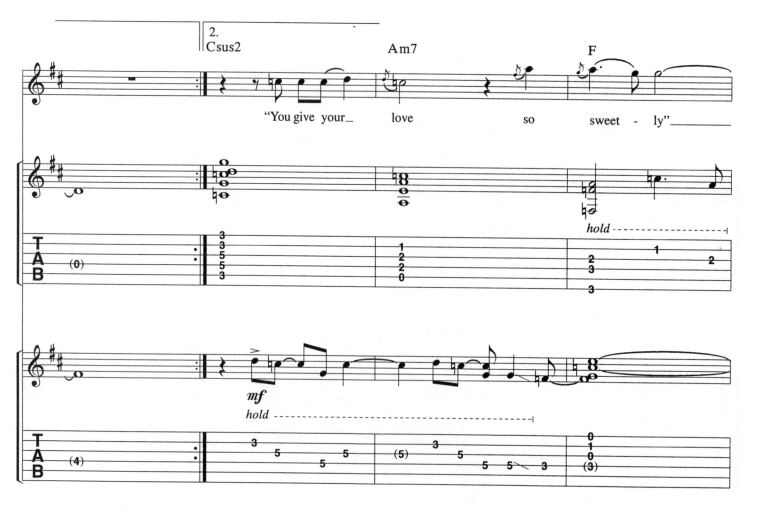

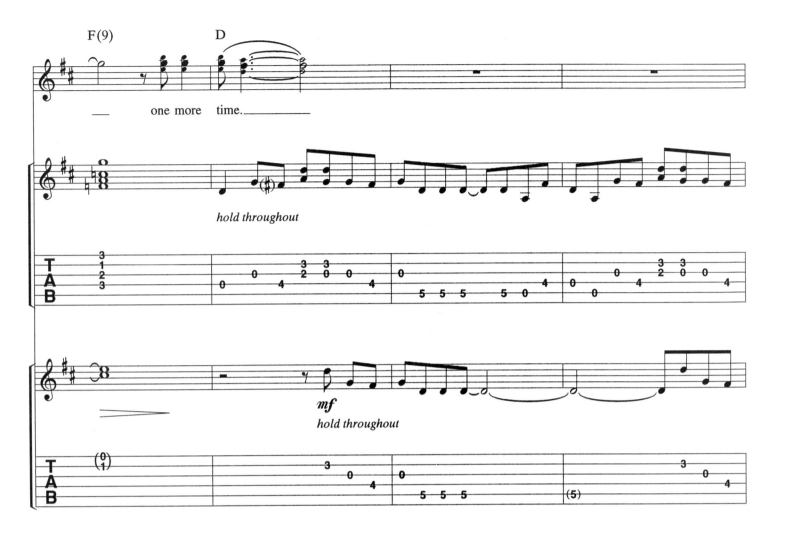

one more time._____

hold throughout

mf

hold throughout

D.S. % al Coda

112

"Oh, my love, my dar - ling_____ I've

w/Rhy. Fig. 1 *(Gtr. 1) 2 1/2 times, simile*

hun - gered for your touch a_____ long,_____ lone - ly time.__

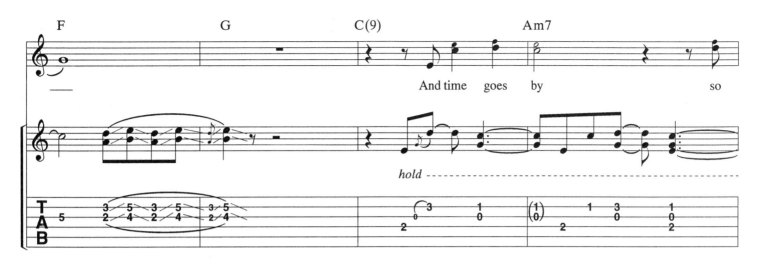

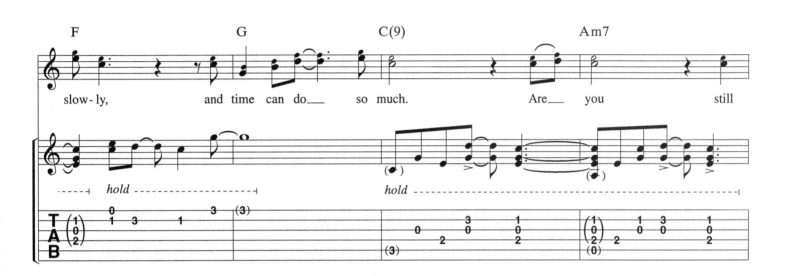

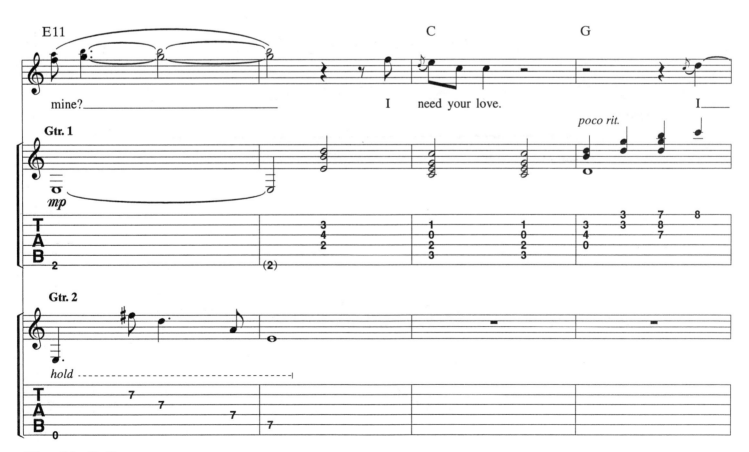

Chinese Cafe - 12 - 10
PG9666

114

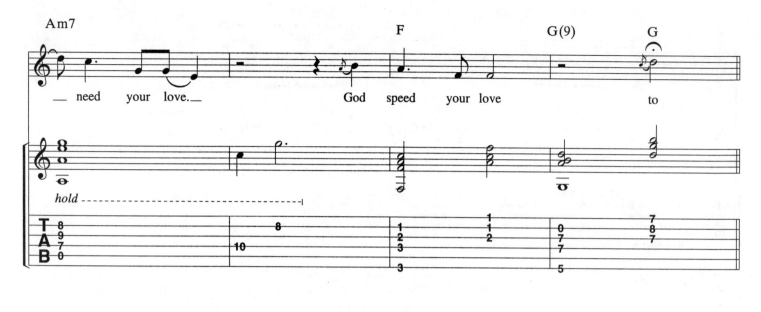

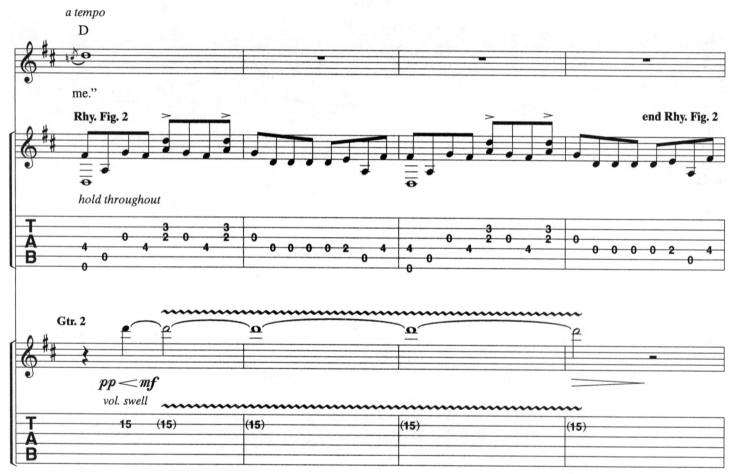

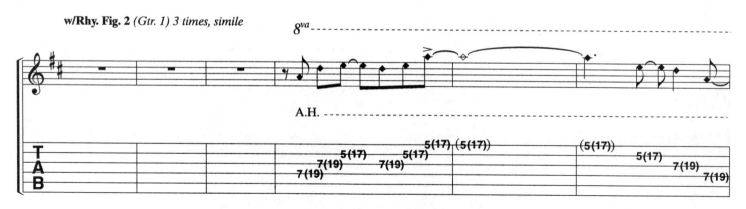

Chinese Cafe - 12 - 11
PG9666

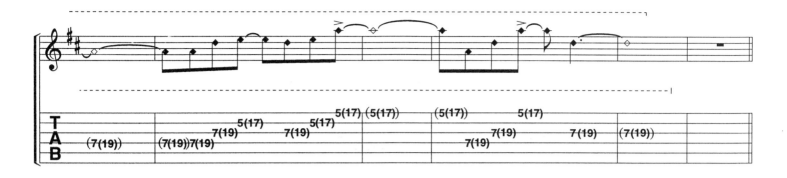

Outro:
w/Rhy. Fig. 2 *(Gtr. 1) simile*

Repeat and fade

Time__ goes._____ Where does the time__ go?_____ I won-der where the...

Gtr. 2

mp

Verse 2:
Uranium money
Is booming in the old home town now.
It's putting up sleek concrete,
Tearing the old landmarks down,
Paving over brave little parks,
Ripping off Indian land again.
How long? How long?
Short-sighted businessmen.
Ah, nothing lasts for long.
Nothing lasts for long.
Nothing lasts for long.
(To Chorus:)

Verse 3:
Christmas is sparkling
Out on Carol's lawn.
This girl of my childhood games
Has kids nearly grown and gone.
Grown so fast
Like the turn of a page.
We look like our mothers did now
When we were those kids' age.
Nothing lasts for long,
Nothing lasts for long,
Nothing lasts for long.
(To Chorus:)

COME IN FROM THE COLD

Words and Music by
JONI MITCHELL

Gtrs. 1 & 2 tune to:

⑥ = D♭ ③ = F

⑤ = F ② = A♭

④ = D♭ ① = D♭

Freely

Intro:

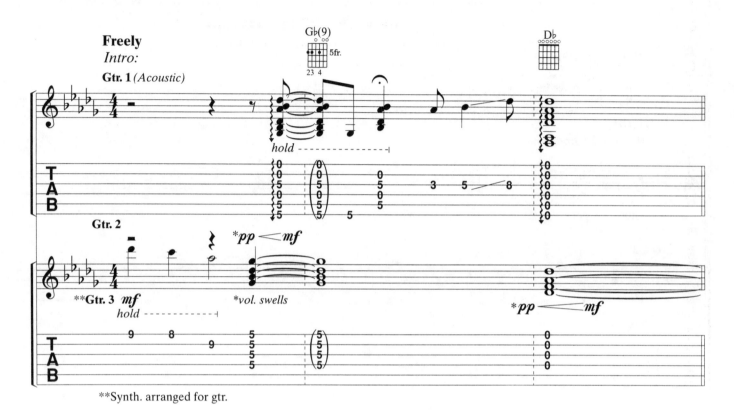

Gtr. 1 *(Acoustic)*

Gtr. 2

**Synth. arranged for gtr.

Moderately ♩ = 108

Verses:

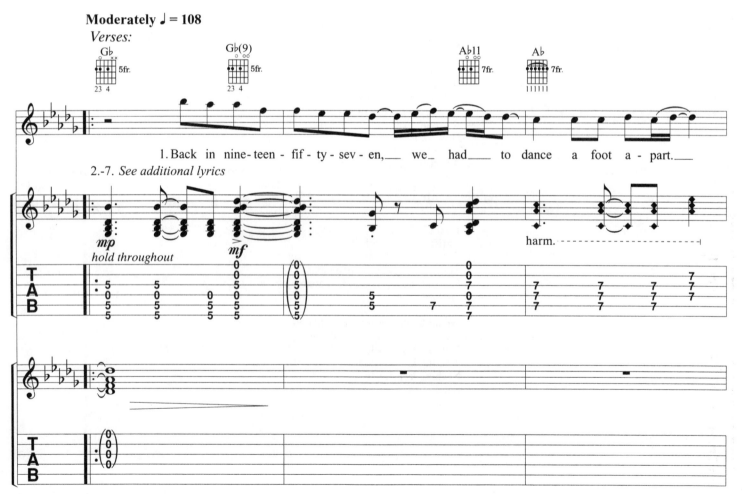

1. Back in nine-teen-fif-ty-sev-en,___ we_ had___ to dance a foot a-part.___

2.-7. *See additional lyrics*

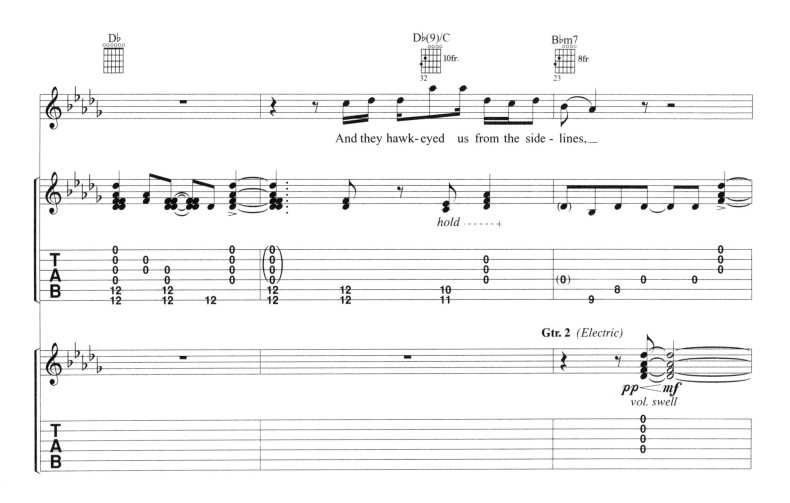

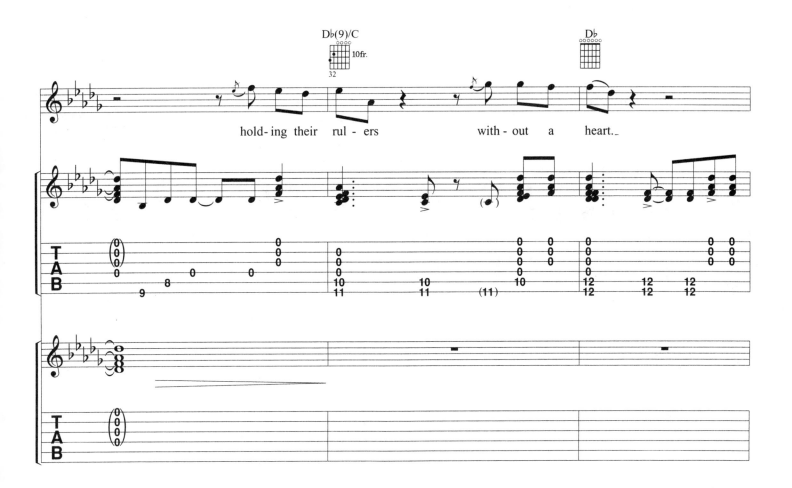

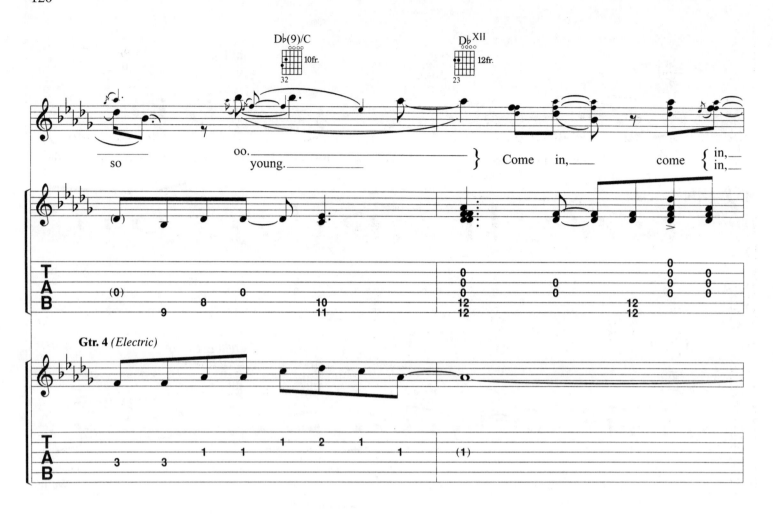

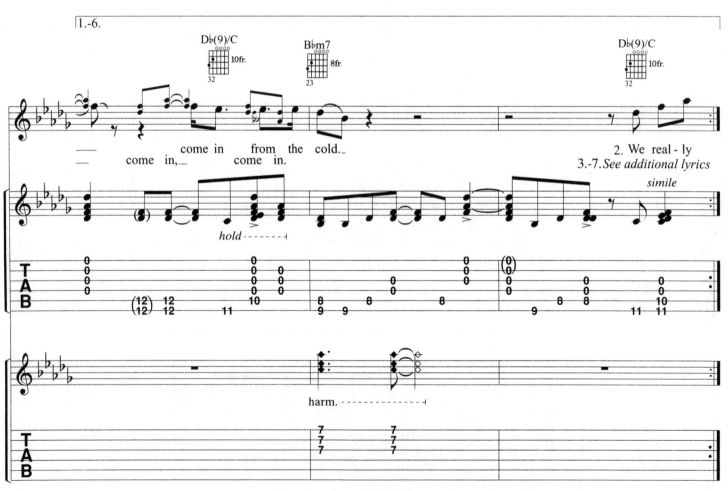

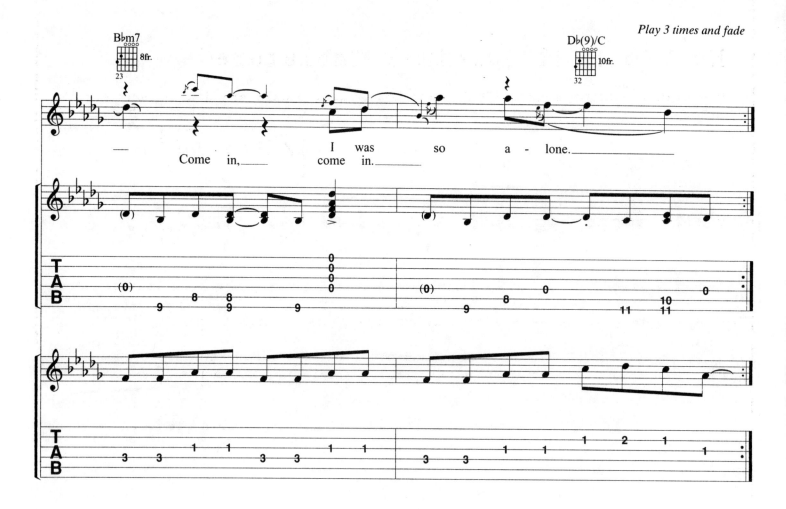

Verse 2:
We really thought we had a purpose,
We were so anxious to achieve.
We had hope,
The world held promise
For a slave
To liberty.
Freely, I slaved away for something better,
And I was bought and sold.
And all I ever wanted
Was just to come in from the cold.

Chorus 2:
Come in,
Come in from the cold.
(We were so sure.)
Please come in,
Come in from the cold.

Verse 3:
I feel your legs under the table,
Leaning into mine.
I feel renewed,
I feel disabled
By these bonfires in my spine.
I don't know who the arsonist was,
Which incendiary soul,
But all I ever wanted
Was just to come in from the cold.

Chorus 3:
Come in,
Come in from the cold.
(You were so warm.)
Oh, come in, come in,
Come in from the cold.

Verse 4:
I am not some stone commission,
Like a statue in a park.
I am flesh and blood and vision,
I am howling in the dark.
Long, blue shadows of the jackals
Are falling on a pay phone
By the road
Oh, all they ever wanted
Was just to come in from the cold.

Chorus 4:
Come in,
Come in from the cold.
(I was so low.)
Oh, come in,
Come in from the cold.

Verse 5:
Is this just vulgar electricity?
Is this the edifying fire?
(It was so pure.)
Does your smile's covert complicity,
Debase as it admires?
(Just a flu with a temperature.)
Are you checking out your mojo,
(Oohoo.)
Or am I just fighting off growing old?
(Just a high fever.)
All I ever wanted
Was just to come in from the cold.

Chorus 5:
Come in,
Oh, come in from the cold.
(It was so pure.)
Please come in,
Come in from the cold.

Verse 6:
I know we will never be perfect,
Never entirely clear.
(When the moon shines.)
We get hurt and we just panic,
And we strike out
Out of fear.
(You were only being kind.)
I fear the sentence of this solitude,
200 years on hold.
(For my loving crime.)
Oh, and all we ever wanted
Was just to come in from the cold.

Chorus 6:
Come in,
Oh, come in from the cold.
(When the moon shines.)
Oh, come in,
Come in from the cold.

Verse 7:
When I thought life had some meaning,
Then I thought I had some choice.
(I was running blind.)
And I made some value judgements
In a self-important voice.
(I was outta line.)
But then absudity came over me,
And I longed to lose control.
(Into no mind.)
Oh, all I ever wanted
Was just to come in from the cold.

Chorus 7:
Come in,
Come in from the cold.
(You were so kind.)
Please come in,
(So kind.)
Come in from the cold.
Come in, come in,
Come in from the cold.

How To Read Dulcimer Tablature

The traditional Appalachian dulcimer has a bass, middle and double course of melody strings:

The bass string is usually a wound string, similar in gauge to a guitar's G string. The middle string is similar to a guitar's high B or E and the double melody strings are also similar to a guitar's high B or E.

↑   An up arrow indicates a strum across all the strings, away from your body, striking the double melody strings first, followed by the middle and bass strings.

↓   A down arrow indicates a strum across all of the strings, toward your body, striking the bass strings first, followed by the middle and double melody strings.

-   A dash represents a rest or pause equal to an eighth note.

T   A "T" indicates a "slap" or muted strum. Strum an up-stroke while simultaneously muting the strings with the palm of your strumming hand. You should hear only a percussive slap.

Dulcimer Strumming Patterns

| ↑ - *T ↓ ↑ - T ↓ | ↑ - T ↓ ↑ ↓ ↑ ↓ | - ↓ - ↓ ↑ - T ↓ |
| up rest slap down up rest slap down | up rest slap down up down up down | rest down rest down up rest slap down |

* T = mute

Attention Guitar Players:

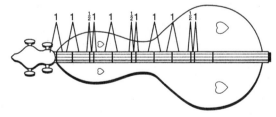

Dulcimers are not fretted chromatically. The frets on a dulcimer form a diatonic pattern of whole- and half-steps. From any open string the pattern is w w h w w h w. This is a mixolydian scale. Starting at the 3rd fret and continuing up the neck to the 10th fret would form a major scale.

GUITAR TAB GLOSSARY **

TABLATURE EXPLANATION

READING TABLATURE: Tablature illustrates the six strings of the guitar. Notes and chords are indicated by the placement of fret numbers on a given string(s).

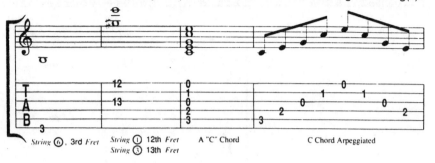

String ⑥, 3rd Fret   String ① 12th Fret   A "C" Chord   C Chord Arpeggiated
String ③ 13th Fret

BENDING NOTES

HALF STEP: Play the note and bend string one half step.*

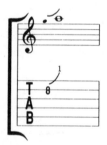

WHOLE STEP: Play the note and bend string one whole step.

PREBEND AND RELEASE: Bend the string, play it, then release to the original note.

RHYTHM SLASHES

STRUM INDICA-TIONS: Strum with indicated rhythm.

The chord voicings are found on the first page of the transcription underneath the song title.

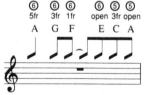

INDICATING SINGLE NOTES USING RHYTHM SLASHES: Very often single notes are incorporated into a rhythm part. The note name is indicated above the rhythm slash with a fret number and a string indication.

*A half step is the smallest interval in Western music; it is equal to one fret. A whole step equals two frets.

**By Kenn Chipkin and Aaron Stang

ARTICULATIONS

HAMMER ON: Play lower note, then "hammer on" to higher note with another finger. Only the first note is attacked.

PULL OFF: Play higher note, then "pull off" to lower note with another finger. Only the first note is attacked.

LEGATO SLIDE: Play note and slide to the following note. (Only first note is attacked).

PALM MUTE: The note or notes are muted by the palm of the pick hand by lightly touching the string(s) near the bridge.

ACCENT: Notes or chords are to be played with added emphasis.

DOWN STROKES AND UPSTROKES: Notes or chords are to be played with either a downstroke (⊓ ·) or upstroke (∨) of the pick.

© 1990 Beam Me Up Music
c/o CPP/Belwin, Inc. Miami, Florida 33014
International Copyright Secured   Made in U.S.A.   All Rights Reserved